INDOOR CLIMBING

TECHNICAL SKILLS FOR CLIMBING WALLS
FOR NOVICES, EXPERTS AND INSTRUCTORS

With information relevant to the
NICAS, CWA and CWLA schemes

ABOUT THE AUTHOR

Pete has climbed in many continents and countries across the world, including first ascents in the Himalayas. He is holder of the MIC award, the highest UK instructional qualification, and has been delivering rock and mountain sports courses at the highest level for a number of years. He is a member of the Alpine Club, Honorary Life Member of the Association of Mountaineering Instructors and a Fellow of the Royal Geographical Society. A lack of common sense has found him on the north faces of the Eiger and Matterhorn in winter, as well as a number of other extreme routes climbed in extreme conditions in the European Alps, Africa, Nepal and India.

Pete lives in Scotland and has two daughters, Rebecca and Samantha. A frequent contributor to various magazines and websites, he is author of *Sport Climbing* and *Rock Climbing*, both for Cicerone Press, as well as *The International Handbook of Technical Mountaineering*, *The Complete Guide to Climbing and Mountaineering* and co-author of the internationally successful *Mountain Skills Training Handbook*. He enjoys route setting, bouldering and dry tooling competitions.

He runs both summer and winter skills courses at all levels and is a course director for a number of UK award courses, including the CWA (Climbing Wall Award) and SPA (Single Pitch Award). He can be contacted via his website at www.petehillmic.com.

Other guides by the author
Sport Climbing (Cicerone)
Rock Climbing (Cicerone)
The Mountain Skills Training Handbook (David & Charles)
The International Handbook of Technical Mountaineering (David & Charles)
The Complete Guide to Climbing and Mountaineering (David & Charles)

INDOOR CLIMBING

TECHNICAL SKILLS FOR CLIMBING WALLS
FOR NOVICES, EXPERTS AND INSTRUCTORS

by

Pete Hill MIC

**With information relevant to the
NICAS, CWA and CWLA schemes**

2 POLICE SQUARE, MILNTHORPE, CUMBRIA, LA7 7PY
www.cicerone.co.uk

Printed by KHL Printing, Singapore
A catalogue record for this book is available from the British Library.

All photographs by the author except those on the following pages, for which I am extremely grateful: 59, 60 Undercover Rock, Bristol; 6, 8, 96 Awesome Walls, Liverpool; 90, 180 Rob Mitchell/Craggy Island, Guildford; 42, 64, 137 Boulders Indoor Climbing, Cardiff; 73 Phil Minal/Redpoint Climbing Centre; 175 Ratho, Edinburgh. *Front cover:* An interesting feature that makes for a tricky lead (Phil Minal/ The Redpoint Climbing Centre)

To Rebecca and Samantha. For all the times we've had together, and those to come.

ACKNOWLEDGEMENTS

As with any project of this size, there are myriad people and venues whose skills, knowledge and climbing sessions I have tapped in to, and to all of these I am greatly indebted: Samantha Hill, Rebecca Hill, Allen Fyffe, Rachel Hutchison, Gemma Callow, Malcolm Lee, Anna Wells, Cara Chamberlain, Gaz Marshall, Sean Cattanach, Caroline Allan, Mike Elliott, Deziree Wilson, Mark Chadwick, Ruairidh MacKenzie, Steve Long at MLT; Rob Aidie at the BMC; Rob Mitchell at Craggy Island, Guildford; David Douglas and Simon Aldridge at Awesome Walls, Liverpool and Stockport; Rob Lawrence at Boulders Indoor Climbing, Cardiff; Nic Crawshaw and Laura Francis at The Adventure Centre, Ratho; Guy Jarvis of NICAS and Undercover Rock, Bristol; Andrew Reid at the ABC; the staff at Glasgow Climbing Centre; Mike Jones and the staff at Calshot, Southampton; Enterprises, The Ice Factor, Kinlochleven; Phil Minal at the Redpoint Climbing Centre, Cardiff; Sieta Whitehead at the Castle Climbing Centre, London; Ali O'Neale at Climbzone, Glasgow; Iain McKenzie at the Tower Climbing Centre, Leicester; The Abernethy Trust and anyone I've missed out who was unlucky enough to get in front of my camera, help out with shots, provide information or send me some pictures to use.

Special thanks go to Scott Muir and Alan Davies at Extreme Dream, Aviemore, who put up with me pottering about taking photographs, moving holds around and generally getting in the way, all with a smile on their faces and frequent offers of a hot cuppa.

The text was technically proof-read by Alan Halewood. Al has a wealth of experience as a manager and technical advisor to some of the UK's most important climbing facilities, and thus was uniquely positioned to point out any inaccuracies and omissions. Thanks Al.

Petzl (www.petzl.com), Beal (www.bealplanet.com) and La Sportiva (www.lasportiva. com) have all provided equipment and technical advice, for which I am very grateful.

Finally, as always, I must thank the long-suffering Paula Griffin, who spent many hours proofreading the text and what must have felt like even longer hours helping with technical photographs. Thanks Paula.

DISCLAIMER

CONTENTS

This book covers techniques for beginners, experts, instructors and group leaders. Some of the techniques are primarily aimed at instructors and group leaders and these sections have been identified with this coloured background. They do contain information that can be important for all climbing wall users so even if you are not an instructor or group leader I recommend that you check out these sections when you are ready for them.

PREFACE

A visit to a climbing wall is no rare occurrence these days. Some years ago walls were seen as simply somewhere to go as a diversion when it was raining, with only a few climbers viewing them as training venues, ideal for practising the skills that would be needed on rock outside.

These days there are people who only *ever* climb indoors, and who see indoor climbing as a sport in its own right. Others use walls purely as training venues, honing the muscles and skills necessary for success on outdoor routes that would otherwise take months of trying to get the right strength and sequences together while dodging showers. Still more will use walls to maintain an overall level of climbing fitness, often for a few hours a couple of evenings a week, enabling them to stay strong until the weekend break lets them get on the rock. And of course there are those who have their first experience of climbing at a wall, in a controlled situation and perhaps with a group of friends, learning about equipment and movement, enjoying the experience together. If all goes well, they will then move on to climb more, both indoors and out, and become regular users of walls for all the right reasons.

The climbing wall environment can feel very sterile to some, and I know a number of climbers who would rather climb in the rain than ever venture inside! However, walls are now a huge and important part of the climbing scene, with the majority of climbers – both those starting out and the more experienced – using walls regularly throughout the year.

It is important that the experience at a wall is enjoyable. Naturally it must also be safe and, ideally, productive but with these factors in place enjoyment should be the next priority. Whether you are training on the hardest of routes or just sampling climbing for the first time, you should be enjoying yourself. Why else would you do it?

With the proliferation of climbing walls comes increased employment, and a significant number of people have jobs connected to the climbing wall business. Many of these are instructors, and the numbers have increased to the extent that the UK now has its own training and assessment programme. The Climbing Wall Award, or CWA, gives the successful candidate a nationally recognised qualification for taking others into the climbing wall environment.

Whatever your reason for going to a wall – simply to experience climbing on an infrequent basis with a couple of friends, as a training facility or as a form of employment – this book should cover everything you need to know.

Pete Hill

Use of colour and angles at Awesome Walls, Liverpool

A section of Awesome Walls, Liverpool

1

CLIMBING WALLS AND STRUCTURES

TYPES

There are many types of climbing walls and other man-made places to climb up or to abseil from, and some of these are outlined below. Much of this book will be looking at standard indoor climbing facilities, but it is worth being aware that other styles of climbing and abseiling venues exist.

Indoor

This will be what most people think of when they talk about climbing walls. Walls have evolved dramatically since the 1970s when they were designed in such a way that simply adding or missing out bricks on the wall at the end of a gymnasium was seen as the way ahead. A process whereby natural rock was incorporated in the wall building, giving climbers the chance to get hold of 'real' rock indoors, eventually gave way to today's very technical, scientifically designed and purpose-built climbing facilities. Walls now go out, up, back and over, with a number even being mechanically operated so that the incline of the wall can be altered to suit the climbing style required at any particular time.

Bolt-on climbing holds, ready to go

Typical early design of a gym-end climbing wall; this one is augmented with extra bolt-on holds

(Above) **One of the huge walls at Ratho Climbing Arena, near Edinburgh**
(Below) **Glasgow Climbing Centre, which makes the most of the original structure of the church**

Outdoor

Some areas sport an outdoor climbing wall. This will again be purpose-built and highly technical in design, with the obvious proviso that rain and cold can sometimes affect whether the wall can be used or not. However, climbing outside is certainly healthier than many indoor environments, as fresh air replaces the slightly chalky and sweaty aroma from which some indoor facilities tend to suffer.

Outdoor climbing wall, built for the climbing World Cup finals

Mobile towers

These are a common sight at fêtes, school functions, shopping
centres and even private homes during parties! Generally consisting of a fibreglass shell, moulded and bolted onto a metal
framework which in turn lays flat on a trailer, the tower can
be towed to where it is needed and erected within minutes.

Usually, a pneumatic or pump system will be used to pivot the tower upright, with outriggers to give it stability.

Belaying is often done with auto-belays, which are mechanical devices that allow the climber to climb up towards them and then be gently lowered to the ground when they jump or fall off. This has the advantage that several climbs can take place simultaneously using just one supervisor, who will be adjusting harnesses and helmets and clipping people on and off, but otherwise will not be involved in the belaying process.

It is possible to bottom-rope from mobile towers, but there is an issue with people standing away from the base causing the structure to become unstable. Thus, auto-belays are the choice of most operators.

Trees

Although this may sound quite odd, a number of outdoor centres use large trees as climbing facilities. These will often have a tree-house-type construction high up, from where an instructor can run a top-rope and abseiling session. Wooden blocks are generally nailed or screwed to the trunk which, along with the branches, enable people to climb.

Looking up at an abseil platform built between a two-trunked tree. Note the ladder for instructors on the left hand trunk

It goes without saying that any construction of this type needs to be professionally built, assessed by a structural engineer and also have a tree surgeon involved in the assessment and completion of the project. However, a tree can provide participants with their first taste of climbing and abseiling wherever there is limited or no access to a climbing wall.

Buildings and structures

This category includes bridges, high-rise buildings, castles and even cranes! Generally used for running abseil sessions, the framework to which any technical equipment is attached needs to have been inspected and passed as fit for purpose by an appropriately qualified person.

An abseiling session run from the roof of a castle

Dry tooling

Dry tooling

This is the use of a pair of specially designed ice axes to progress across what can be the most outrageous-looking ground imaginable! The axes hook onto small holds or into pre-drilled wooden blocks, and the climber then uses the wedged tools to make progress.

Extremely tiring and technical, dry tooling is used by some climbers in the summer months as training for winter climbs. However, it has become a sport in its own right and many walls now have areas dedicated to dry tooling, usually roped off or otherwise segregated from the rest of the climbing wall (see Chapter 10).

Construction of a wall at Ratho near Edinburgh, currently the world's largest indoor climbing arena

WALL CONSTRUCTION

Walls are built from a variety of materials, including wood, metal, plastic and resins. How a wall is built will often depend upon how much money has been spent on its construction by the facility. Two of the commonest types of wall are those with a plywood base onto which holds are fixed with 'T' nuts or similar, and those that have moulded plastic or resin panels bolted into place, again with the facility for affixing holds wherever needed.

Some walls will have a metal substructure onto which the panels are bolted. This enables the designers to give the wall a variety of interesting shapes, angles and features, and allows many more possibilities in design than a simple wooden framework, as it can bear greater weight (such as has to be taken when constructing overhangs).

Anything other than a small wall – which may be built at home in a garage or a spare room in the house – requires skilled design, planning and construction techniques. We need to know that the panels are going to stay in place once we start hanging on them!

The internal framework of one of the walls at Ratho; the holes are where holds are attached

Wall features and holds

Since the introduction of climbing walls in the mid-1970s designers and manufacturers have made huge strides in working out what is possible to keep us amused at a wall. Slabs, roofs, huge overhangs, contoured features and even walls that tilt to suit the occasion are now commonplace. The type of hold used has also come on in leaps and bounds, from the original brick edges to today's myriad pockets, crimps, slopers, jugs, rails, volumes, tufas and more.

(Right) **Large jug**
(Far right) **Small crimp**

(Right) **A sculpted wall that gives good friction for the feet and a number of 'natural'-feeling holds for the hands and fingers**

(Below) **A tufa, which represents a limestone formation, requires strong arms and good technique**

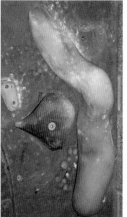

This 'Twiglet' feature requires unusual climbing techniques!

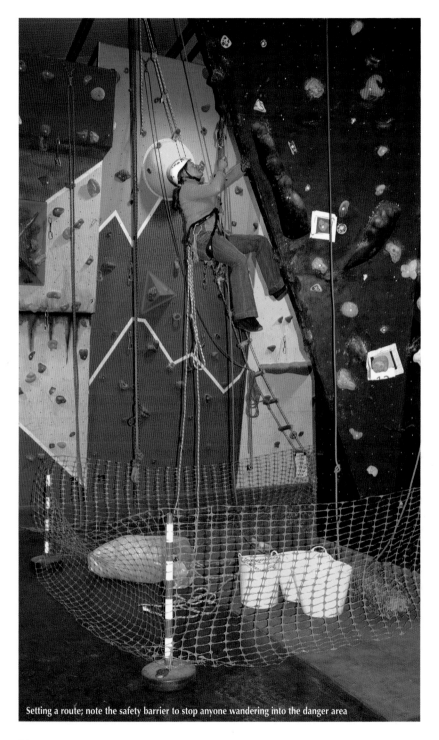
Setting a route; note the safety barrier to stop anyone wandering into the danger area

ROUTE SETTING

This is a skilled job that requires a lot of climbing experience in order for the route setter – who may be a professional setter, one of the wall staff or a part-time setter doing it for enjoyment – to be capable of putting up routes that are appropriate to the grade.

For instance, it would be very difficult for someone whose top-climbing grade is 6a to put up a 7+ on a large overhang, as they will never have experienced that type of climbing at that grade. Thus, they would not be able to come up with the sequence of moves that would be needed to get up such tricky ground, as the route would need to 'flow' in the correct manner to make it both climbable and fun. Route setters also need to be aware that they may put up a lot of routes that encompass their own favourite style of climbing, rather than varying the type of climbing to suit all tastes.

Something else that the route setter needs to be aware of is height. I always take this into account when route setting because, at 6ft 6in tall, my reach is far greater than that of many other wall users! Thus I have to 'think shorter' when setting, otherwise many of my routes would be impossible for people of a more average height to get up.

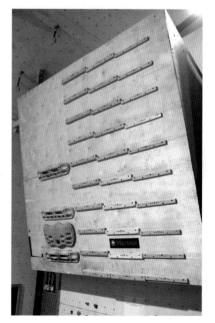

Campus board with various combinations possible

Campus boards

Campus boards, often seen in the corners of climbing walls, will normally be designed to allow just the fingers to be used. As a training device they take up little room but can produce good results if used correctly. They should, however, only be used by experienced climbers and even then only after a thorough warm-up session. Campussing of any type involves using the hands only with feet hanging free, a very demanding and difficult method of training.

Bachar ladder

Named after a training technique developed and promoted by the American John Bachar, the 'Bachar ladder' is a tough method of training (predominantly) the arm muscles. It is typically a rope ladder with wooden rungs, the bottom anchored to the floor and the top anchored some distance away so

Bachar ladder

that the ladder overhangs by 20 degrees or so. The climber climbs up it hand over hand with feet hanging free, then down and back up as often as the training schedule dictates. Repetitions of a small number of ascents are common. As with campus boards, a Bachar ladder should only be used when the climber is completely warmed up. Injuries to the arms and back are not uncommon; because the ladder will swing slightly the climber has to use a greater degree of body control and tension to progress up the rungs.

CLIMBING AT THE WALL

So, how do we set about climbing?

- You will notice that walls generally have a series of coloured holds all over them. The colours denote different route grades or difficulties (see table below), some easy and some hard. A list of routes, the colour and grades, is usually placed at the bottom of each route or on a larger board mounted nearby.

- If there is a rope hanging down and you like the look of that area to climb in, the first thing to do is to find out the rope or panel number. This will be painted on or labelled either at the top or the bottom of that specific route: let's say in this instance it is panel number 15.

- Next, you need to find the route descriptions for panel 15, either at the base of the climb or on the noticeboard nearby. There may be three or four routes listed for each panel, with a different colour noted alongside each route. For instance, there may be a yellow, red, blue and green route, and each of these will have a corresponding number. These numbers give the grade of the route, and denote how hard the climbing will be.

- Generally, the higher the number the harder the route, so you may find that the yellow route on panel 15 is graded 4+, whereas the green route on the same panel is given 6a, making it a harder climb. This will all make a lot more sense when you understand the grading system and have climbed a few routes to find out at which grade you are the most comfortable.

- Assuming that you are going to be doing the yellow route, the climb will be a 4+ graded climb so long as you only use the yellow holds and no others. Wall features, such as small ripples in the surface, are often allowed, but may only be of use for your feet. If no features are allowed in addition to the yellow holds, it will say so on the route description.

Of course there is nothing to stop you using whatever hold you like (using a mixture of holds is called a 'rainbow' route), but if you are up for a challenge then do your best to stay with the one colour. If routes have been set correctly, you should enjoy the climbing, learn a lot about movement and be able to progress through the grades.

GRADES

The French grading system is generally used at walls. This comes from sport climbing, where bolts are pre-placed in the rock and extenders clipped in as the climber progresses. This is different from 'traditional' climbing, where the leader places a variety of protection devices into the rock, which are removed by the second person to ascend. As all the protection on climbing walls is in place, the French system is used. The

> **Note**
>
> Each wall will have its own colour and numbering conventions so check these out carefully before climbing.

Route grade card, usually found at the bottom of walls

only time that this may not be the case is where leader-placed protection can be used, and here the standard UK grading system will be the one indicated.

The table below shows the comparison between UK and French grades. Only the standard 'bench-mark' UK grades are shown, as there can be a little leeway between adjacent grades. Many climbers starting out at the wall will be able to climb up to grade 4; routes graded much higher than that start to require some technique and a bit of strength.

UK Traditional Grades	French Grading System
Moderate	1
Difficult	2
Very Difficult 3a	2+
Hard Very Difficult 3b	3-
Mild Severe 3c	3
Severe 4a	3+
Hard Severe 4b	3+, 4
Mild Very Severe	4
Very Severe 4c	4, 4+
Hard Very Severe 5a	5, 5+
E1 5b,	5+, 6a
E2 5c	6a+, 6b
E3 6a	6b, 6b+
E4 6a/b	6c, 6c+, 7a
E5 6b	7a, 7a+, 7b
E6 6b/c	7b+, 7c, 7c+
E7 6c/7a	7c+, 8a, 8a+
E8 6c/7a	8a+, 8b, 8b+
E9 7a/b	8b+, 8c, 8c+
E10 7a/b	9a+, 9b, 9b+

Leading across the huge roof at Extreme Dream, Aviemore

Leading steep ground at Craggy Island; note the group below wearing helmets

2 EQUIPMENT

One of the great things about climbing indoors is the minimal amount of equipment required. If you don't own any kit it's not a problem; larger facilities often hire out rock boots, harness, helmet, belay device and karabiner. However, you will almost certainly want to accumulate your own kit over time, and the following list gives a few pointers as to what kit may be appropriate for use indoors. Equipment specific to dry tooling is given in Chapter 10.

Rock boots
This is the most important piece of kit and probably the first item you will purchase. It is also one of the most expensive, so buying correctly first time will save you a lot of bother and money.

Although the term 'boots' is frequently used, this also covers 'shoes' and 'slippers'. These names generally refer to the difference in the height of fit above or below the ankle, the decision about which to buy being mainly down to personal preference.

This is one piece of kit where a trip down the high street – rather than going for an Internet purchase – will be a good idea. A well-stocked shop and a helpful and knowledgeable assistant are needed, as the myriad makes and types of shoe available will take some time to try on and consider.

Think about the following when trying on rock boots:

- **Comfort** Do not heed the advice that your shoes should be two or three sizes too small, causing you to hobble around the climbing wall with tears in your eyes. A snug fit without socks is important (make sure that your toenails are short when trying boots on), as this will give you control over foot placement on small holds and edges. If the boot is too large the side will roll off the smallest holds.

- **Fit** Ensure that there are no gaps around your foot, particularly at the toe and heel sections. A number of shops will have a small section of wall on which you can balance so that you can feel how the boots perform.

Lace-up *(left)* **and Velcro closure boot**

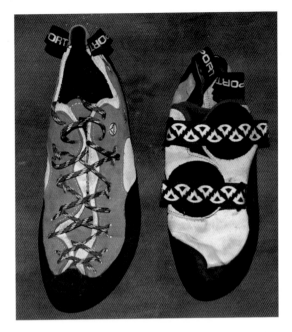

- **Laces or straps?** Boots come with either laces or Velcro straps. The choice is up to you, but unless the fit of the boot is perfect and the Velcro is just being used to hold it in place around your foot, most people find that laces give far more control in making the boot fit well.

- **Soles** All rock boots come with 'sticky' rubber soles, and there is little to choose between them in performance.

To sum up: go for a boot (shoe or slipper), that is comfortable when worn, is snug enough to give you control over foot placement, has no gaps inside and secures around your foot efficiently.

Instructor's note

The use of outdoor footwear is not allowed on many walls. This is primarily for reasons of health and safety, as footwear that has been worn in the street may deposit dirt and bacteria on holds that will later be used by hands. If you are taking a group to a climbing facility check the in-house policy and ensure that you have enough rock boots to go round, or are able to hire them.

Chalk bag

This piece of kit is not essential to start with, but as you progress through the grades you will find it useful to have one with you. The 'chalk' (magnesium carbonate) is supplied in block, powder or ball form. A dusting of chalk on your fingers gives a little extra grip and helps to dry up any moisture caused by finger-pad perspiration.

Two types of chalk bag are commonly used:

- Tied around you or clipped to your harness and carried up the route

- A much larger version, left on the ground as a 'base-camp' bag, into which you can dip at regular intervals. The advantage of the latter is that, when bouldering (see Chapter 5), you do not keep falling onto a bag tied around your waist with the inevitable result of clouds of chalk being propelled into the atmosphere!

Chalk 'balls' – loose chalk contained within a very fine meshed fabric – are often the only form of chalk permitted on many walls. You simply tap or rub your fingers on the fabric to get a coating of chalk. Chalk balls are preferred because they do not create a lot of dust, which is harmful to breathe in and annoying to many users as everything becomes coated in a fine white film.

There is also a resinous substance available that is applied from a bottle to your fingertips; it dries them out, giving a sticky feel. However, the use of this is frowned on at some walls as it can clog up the grain on climbing holds. Climbers generally seem to prefer the feel of chalk, not least because of the therapeutic act of chalking up while hanging off a route, pondering the way ahead.

Chalk bag *(left)* and 'base-camp' bag

Harness

Rock boots and chalk bag get you bouldering; a harness will get you climbing. As with boots, there is a bewildering variety of types, shapes, sizes and functions to look at, so the following pointers will hopefully help.

- If the harness is just going to be used indoors, choose one **without adjustable leg loops**. These are handy if you are going to be venturing outside, as the harness can be adjusted to fit over different thicknesses of clothing. However, indoors you are likely to be wearing thin trousers and perhaps a light fleece, so a high degree of adjustability is not necessary. The leg loops should not be too tight; being able to push your hand comfortably down between the leg loop and your thigh shows that it is about right.

- Choose one with an **abseil loop** at the front central point. This small very strong piece of sewn tape will be used for belaying from, as well as being a connecting point for abseiling.

- Reasonable **padding** around the thighs and across the back is a good idea, particularly if you are keen to try to push your grade (in which case you may be taking a bit of 'flying time'!).

- Although not a prime consideration a few **gear loops** for carrying gear – belay device, spare karabiner and perhaps a number of extenders – are a good idea. Make sure that these are arranged appropriately to the side and do not get in the way of the front of the harness.

A good wall harness, with fixed leg loops and auto-locking waist belt

As with boots, a harness purchase requires you to try on a few so that you are happy with the fit. There are slight differences between ladies' and gents' harnesses, in particular the distance between the waist belt and the leg loops. Find that shop with the helpful assistant again, and plan to spend a while in there!

A child's harness and adult's chest harness

BUYING A HARNESS FOR A CHILD

When considering a harness for a child an important consideration comes into play: because children have a different centre of gravity to adults, and because their hips are not always particularly pronounced, there is a concern that they could fall out of a standard sit-harness if they become inverted. The harness could also work its way down over their waist as they climb. Thus, for a child of up to around 10 or 12 years of age a full body harness would be best. These are made specifically with children in mind and are available in a variety of sizes, also being adjustable within those size ranges. The attachment point is usually a tie-in system at chest height, positioned so that the wearer would always end up vertical in the event of a fall.

Another option would be to use a chest harness with a standard sit-harness. The chest harness slips over the shoulders and is linked into the normal tie-on knot, thus creating a system that is impossible to fall out of.

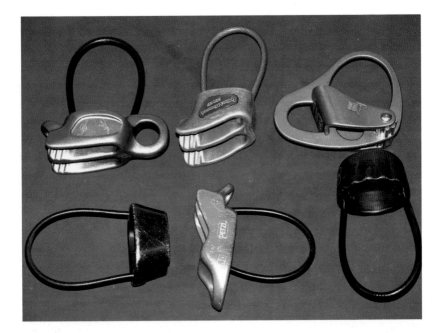

Slick belay devices

Belay device

This is an essential piece of kit and it is important to think carefully prior to purchase to ensure you buy the best type for your particular climbing style and needs.

Belay devices can be separated into two main categories:

- Those that are reasonably **slick** and require you to hold the rope strongly to control a fall; and
- Those that are **self-locking** and which take a little more practice and care in controlling the rope.

All varieties of the first type look fairly similar, and usually consist of a metal plate or bucket shape with two slots, with an attached wire carrying cable. Many have a tapering groove by each slot, which helps to control thinner climbing ropes. The advantage of this type of device is that it works as both an abseil and a belay device, so if you are also going to be climbing out of doors this type would be your most likely choice. Another important factor is that you can provide 'dynamic' belaying (see Chapter 6).

The second type is more technical and takes more practice, especially when paying out to a leader. It is also more difficult to provide a dynamic brake when holding a leader fall, as this type is designed to grip the rope when a load is applied. Although it will (usually!) lock off automatically, it

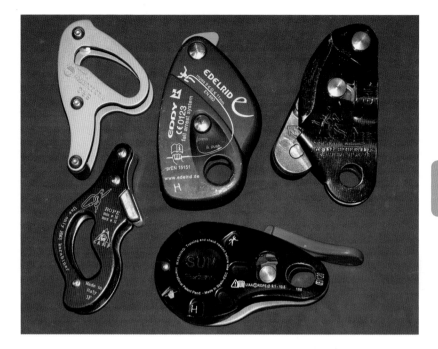

is by no means a 'hands off' device, and the rope still needs to be carefully managed. Only one rope can be used with a self-locking device, so it is less versatile than a slick belay device.

Some climbers will start their careers by using one of the slick devices, and then progress to a self-locking device. This logical progression allows you to learn the basics of belaying before moving on to more technical pieces of kit. There is also a financial consideration: slick devices cost around a third of the price of the self-locking variety. The use of these various devices is covered in Chapters 7 and 8.

Self-locking belay devices

Screwgate karabiners
You will only need a couple of screwgate karabiners, one for your belay device and a spare to use with a sling (see below). The one for your belay device should be a 'pear-shaped' or 'HMS' screwgate, which has a large curve to its bottom end. This will allow you to use the belay device without the rope jamming (if using a slick device). If you are using a self-locking device, a 'D'-shaped screw gate is often recommended to ensure that the device sits correctly. For your sling a D-shape karabiner will suffice.

Pear-shape or HMS karabiner
(left) **and D-shape karabiner**

Slings

A sling of 120cm (sometimes called an '8-foot' sling) may be useful. In particular, it can be used to connect you or your belayer to any ground anchor that is available. This can be attached to the abseil loop on your harness by means of a lark's foot knot (see Chapter 6), with the karabiner on the other end of the sling being clipped in to the anchor.

Rope

At most modern climbing facilities a number of bottom ropes will already be in place. However, you may wish to progress to leading, so owning your own rope would be desirable.

Some manufacturers make specific wall ropes. These come in lengths of 30m or so, with a diameter of 10.5 or 10.2mm, constructed in such a way that they are resilient to the rough handling that a wall rope has to endure. They can be used for both leading and bottom-roping.

Most climbing ropes that are designated as 'single' ropes (tested and approved to be used alone without another rope having to be used alongside) can be used at climbing walls.

It is worth understanding the difference between the two main rope types: 'dynamic', and 'static' or 'low-stretch'.

Dedicated wall rope, designed to withstand heavy use

• A **dynamic rope** will stretch for a percentage of its length when loaded, such as when you hold a leader fall. This is a very important property as the rope absorbs energy that would otherwise be transmitted to the leader, who could sustain injury if they stopped falling too quickly.

• A **low-stretch rope** does not have the elongation properties of a dynamic rope, thus a leader taking a fall onto one of these would almost certainly have a very uncomfortable experience, as well as a chance of sustaining injury.

Only dynamic ropes should be used when in a lead situation.

For all other uses, such as bottom- or top-roping and when rigging abseils, a low-stretch rope would be adequate. Indeed, many *in situ* bottom ropes at climbing walls will be of the low-stretch variety, as they are more resilient to harsh wear and are cheaper to replace. Having said that, other walls will use dynamic ropes as bottom ropes in case climbers pull them through and lead with them. They are also more comfortable to fall on to, particularly if there is some slack in the system.

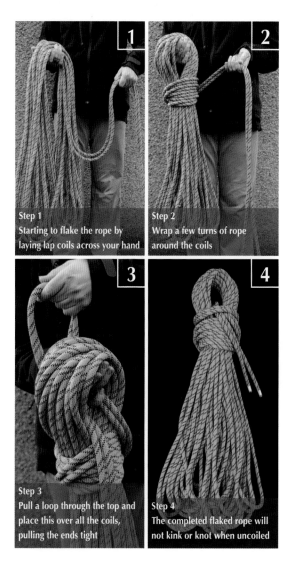

Step 1
Starting to flake the rope by laying lap coils across your hand

Step 2
Wrap a few turns of rope around the coils

Step 3
Pull a loop through the top and place this over all the coils, pulling the ends tight

Step 4
The completed flaked rope will not kink or knot when uncoiled

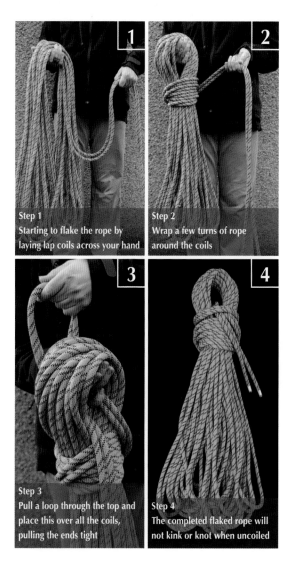

If you do not have a rope bag, you may wish to carry your rope in a more conventional manner. This is known as 'flaking' the rope, and is a very common way to carry it. The pictures show how it is done, and once finished you will be able to carry the rope under a rucksack lid or in a holdall. To unflake it, remove the loop from the top and unwrap the short coils from around the flakes. Hold on to one end and put the rest of the rope on the floor. Keeping the end to one side, run the rope all the way through until you get to the other end. The climber will tie on to the end of the rope coming out from the top of the pile.

Note

Make sure that you unflake the rope where you need it to be. There is no point in undoing a rope by the lockers, only to have to drag it across the floor to beneath your climb!

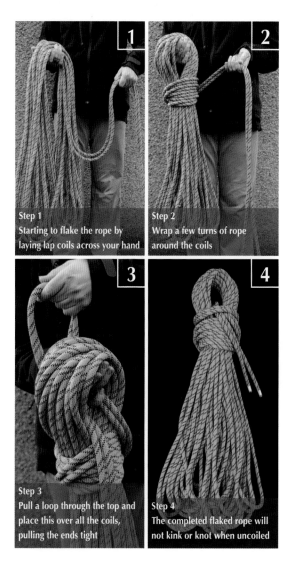 *(EQUIPMENT — chapter tab 2)*

Rope bag with mat extended

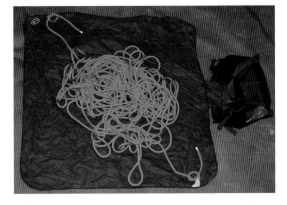

Rope bag

Although not essential – and obviously not needed if you do not have your own rope – a rope bag not only provides a means of carrying the rope but also opens out into a large sheet onto which you can lay your rope when climbing. The advantage is that, once you have led one route and pulled the rope back down, you can simply pick up the sheet and move it to the base of the next climb, which avoids having to drag the rope around on the ground.

Extenders

Some climbing walls have the facility for you to lead routes while placing your own extenders into the bolt hangers that are already *in situ*. Most walls have the extenders (or 'quick-draws'), already in position, but having your own may give you the opportunity to climb in quieter sections of the wall at busy times.

Extenders are short lengths of sewn tape with a snapgate karabiner at each end, often one straight gate and one bent gate. The straight gate is always clipped to the bolt; the bent gate is reserved exclusively for use on the rope end of the system. The shape of the gate allows the rope to be clipped in a little easier when making a quick clip during a hard move (you'll notice that lots of *in situ* extenders at climbing walls have bent gates on them). Extender length tends to be around 15–20cm, and some climbers like a mix of short and long. My personal preference for indoors is a set 15cm long.

The gates can be either solid or wire in design. The advantage of the wire gates – apart from weighing less – is that the gate is less prone to vibration in the event of a fall, meaning that the karabiner is less likely to be in a 'gate open' mode when the weight of a leader comes on to it. This is an important consideration when climbing outside and where the length of a fall could be considerable. However,

Note

. . . .

Some walls do not allow this style of lead-ing, so you will have to check the situation at each wall that you wish to use.

in a climbing wall environment and with the frequency of good, solid bolt placements, this is not a real concern.

Helmet

Many – I would venture the vast majority – of climbing wall users never use a helmet (unless undertaking a dry tooling session, where they are usually compulsory). The climbing wall environment makes you feel safe and 'bomb-proof', so free from danger – or so you think. Falling from a route when leading, swinging across if slipping on a bottom rope, other climbers falling on you and dropping gear on your head… there are many reasons why a helmet is a good idea.

At many walls, where in-house courses are run, participants will be required to wear a helmet while under instruction, and at a number of walls helmets have to be worn at all times by under 18s.

Helmets can often be borrowed or hired from reception desks. If you are thinking about also climbing outdoors then you may want to purchase your own, and could then decide when and when not to wear it.

Helmets are lightweight and comfortable; gone are the days of having something akin to a coal scuttle on your head! However, as heads are different shapes, and helmets will not only sit differently but will feel different to each person, it's back to that helpful person at the shop again!

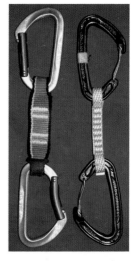

Extender with a solid straight gate *(left – upper)* **and bent gate karabiner** *(left – lower)*, **and one with two straight wire gates** *(right)*

HELMETS FOR CHILDREN

Helmets specifically designed for children are also available and well worth using. Placing an adult's helmet on a child's head is not good, because it will not adjust properly and the constant movement of the cradle while climbing will put the wearer off using one for ever. A proper child's helmet is lightweight, comfortable and has a cradle system that will adjust down to a small head size for a good fit.

Three styles of lightweight helmet

3

WARMING UP (AND DOWN)

Equipment for specific finger- and wrist-warming exercises: a tennis ball that can be squeezed, a gyroscope for wrists and arms, sprung finger exercisers and power putty that provides resistance when squeezed by the fingers

Most climbers recognise this as an essential part of their climbing session. Correct warming up helps to reduce the chance of injury as well as increasing the chance of performing well as your body, as well as your mind, is prepared for exercise. Ignoring a warming-up session, or simply spending a few moments swinging your arms in the air, is asking for trouble: a popped tendon or finger pulley injury could keep you away from climbing for six months or more. So, even though you may feel bulletproof (and the younger you are the more likely you are to think this), don't believe it and get a warm-up routine sorted out before a serious injury stops you from climbing altogether.

WHY WARM UP?

Imagine a car on a very cold morning. If you start it up and drive off straight away, its performance will be very poor for the first couple of miles until it has warmed up properly, and there is the chance that over-exerting it could cause some sort of mechanical failure. However, if you give it a couple of minutes or so in the drive to warm up, it will respond far better when out on the road and the chance of a cold component in the engine failing is dramatically reduced. The human body is remarkably similar.

A simple routine is all that is needed, and will typically consist of three elements:

- **Aerobic activity** Increasing your breathing rate and heartbeat helps your muscles to warm up and become prepared for exercise. Anything that gets you panting and your heart pumping – a run around the car park a few times, a jogging and jumping session or something similar – will do the trick. The best way is a few minutes with the old-fashioned (but never surpassed) skipping rope; 30 seconds of standing still and jiggling your arms will not do the job!

- **Joint-loosening exercises** Mobilising your joints helps to prepare them for exercise. Start with your ankles and rotate them 10 times one way and then the other, working up to your knees, hips, waist, shoulders, elbows, wrists and fingers. Working your finger joints is important; squeeze a tennis ball, use a sprung finger exerciser or even special training putty, designed to be non-sticky and malleable, to provide resistance exercise to your fingers. Another useful tool is an exercise gyroscope, which warms up and strengthens your wrist and arm muscles. These finger exercises can be done while you carry out the rest of the routine. Don't overexert or overstretch, and never stretch any part of your body unless it has been warmed up beforehand.

- **Sport-specific activity** Bouldering or climbing very easy routes is the best way to do this, but try to make your movements very deliberate and choose big holds to start with, and take four times longer for each move than you would normally. This will not only help you prepare physically for the forthcoming climbing session, it will also help you to become attuned mentally.

There is no set time period for the warming-up section of your session, and every person will be different, but treating about a third of your overall climbing time as the warm-up is often seen as being the right amount. This warm-up time, maybe an hour out of a three-hour wall session, will also include bouldering and climbing easy routes, and you will then be well prepared to climb harder and push yourself on more technical ground.

FINGER RACING

This is a good way of showing why a warm-up routine is beneficial to your muscles and joints prior to exercise. I often use it when working with trainee instructors who want to demonstrate the benefit of a warm-up to their clients.

Make a fist with both hands and put your index fingers up. Now have a race; flex and extend each finger as fast as possible simultaneously. One will probably feel much easier to move than the other (often the right finger if you are right-handed and vice versa). Stop after a few seconds. Hold the stiffest finger in the other hand and give it a good rub to warm it, rub the joint a bit, gently pull it, and give it a good warming session. Now start the finger race start again. You should find that the rubbed and stretched finger moves far easier than the other now that it has been prepared for exercise.

'Juggy' routes are a good
way to continue your warm-up

THE BENEFITS OF WARMING UP

A correct warm-up procedure has many benefits; some are listed below.

- Blood flow to all parts of the body is increased.
- The viscosity of blood is decreased, making it flow more easily.
- An increase in body temperature increases the speed and quality of the passage of oxygen around the body, as warm red blood cells are more efficient at carrying oxygen than cold.
- Blood flow to the skeletal system is increased, from an estimated 20 percent at rest to around 70 percent when correctly warmed up.
- Production of synovial fluid is increased, essential to reduce friction between joints.
- Muscle temperature is increased.
- Muscles become less stiff and able to move more freely; tissues become more elastic.
- Energy is supplied through the breakdown of glycogen.
- Nerve conductivity is increased.
- Nerve sensitivity is increased.
- The speed of nerve impulses, thus reaction time, is increased.
- The ability to grip is increased.
- The chance of musculoskeletal injury is reduced.
- The efficient supply of blood to the heart for the activity about to take place is increased.
- The chance of hypoxia is decreased and blood pressure reduced.
- Mental agility is increased.
- The climber becomes more mentally prepared for exercise.

Stretching

Sportsmen and women use a number of stretching techniques to prepare their bodies for exercise. These include the following:

- **Ballistic stretching** A bouncing movement, which has been cited as the cause of many injuries and is not recommended.

- **Static stretching** Commonly seen; a stretch of a body part is taken to the point of mild discomfort and held for 10 to 30 seconds. Overdoing a static stretch can cause injury.

- **PNF stretching** The deliciously named 'proprioceptive neuromuscular facilitation' generally employs a partner to increase the stretch, in particular when working with the legs. This style of stretching is popular where a high degree of flexibility is required, as with some martial arts. Overstretching is easy unless you are careful.

- **Dynamic stretching** This contains elements of the sport for which you are preparing, often done in an exaggerated manner, such as the slow-time bouldering mentioned above. This style of stretching is usually seen to be the most advantageous for climbing.

Recent studies have shown that excessive stretching prior to exercise does not reduce the chance of injury during the exercise phase. Indeed, many injuries have occurred during the warm-up period when too much stress has been put on muscles and tendons before they have been properly prepared for exercise. Some very specific sports, such as martial arts and gymnastics, require a stretching regime in order to complete the discipline. For climbing, dynamic activity-based stretching with low loading and impact on the musculoskeletal system, such as slow-motion bouldering, is to be recommended.

ONGOING ACTIVITY
So, you've warmed up and you're ready for exercise. You meet a pal and have a chat, get geared up and belay your mate for the first route. Chances are that you've now been standing around for 20 minutes and started to cool down, particularly if the facility is chilly in winter. Wearing a hat and warm fleece will help to keep your body warm for a while, but if you are inactive for an extended period don't be tempted to climb on the most desperate route available without having a little extra warm-up to remind your body what you are going to do.

Warming up correctly is essential before moving on to hard boulder problems

YOUNG GROUPS

The specifics of why a warming-up session is important is often lost on younger participants. For instance, if you try to make them do star jumps for five minutes you'll have a mutiny on your hands! However, you can get them warmed up in a fun way. The following activities have been designed so that most areas of the body are used at some point, and core temperature will be raised, allowing for easier movement and helping to avoid soft tissue injuries. Most of these require a lack of self-consciousness in whoever is running the session, along with a keen group.

In the jungle

- Stand in a large circle facing inwards. Explain that you are walking in the jungle; start walking on the spot.

- Tell them that you can hear something behind you, so walk a bit quicker. You now realise that it's a lion, so you have to run!

- Good, there's a lake ahead and lions don't like swimming, so you dive in and start swimming slowly (all mimic the breast-stroke action).

- You hear a noise behind you so you swim on your back (with arms going in an appropriate direction) while you have a look. After a few moments you realise that it's a crocodile! Turn over quickly and start a very fast front crawl.

- Here comes the bank so out you jump; you don't want to hang around, so start running, jumping over lots of fallen trees on the way.

Add to, lengthen or shorten the story as you wish.

Trolley dash

- Fantastic, we are going on holiday! Our flight leaves soon and we need to get some supermarket shopping before we go. Start pushing an imaginary supermarket trolley, jogging lightly in a circle or, if space is limited, on the spot.

- Ah, beans, we need lots of those! Reach out with the right hand and put about 20 tins into your trolley while still moving.

WARMING UP (AND DOWN)

- Tins of spaghetti on the left – 20 of those would be good. Look at your watch and realise that you need to get to the airport, so start jogging faster.

- Breakfast cereal on the right-hand bottom shelf very low down – about five boxes will do.

- On the left at the bottom is milk, perhaps five of those. Chocolate, that would be nice! It's up on the highest shelf on the right, so you have to jump up as you run past, seven bars would be ideal! Now high up on the left, a different type of chocolate, seven of those would balance things up nicely!

- Now to the checkout: run really fast to stop that other person getting there before you! Scan all your shopping; with your right hand get the shopping from the trolley, swing it across in front of you and into your left hand, then drop it into another trolley to your side.

- Pay and push the new trolley out really fast. Get to the car and unpack your 10 bags with both hands and push them up high onto a roof-rack, jumping to get them there.

Again, add or subtract to this depending upon space, time and exhaustion!

Stuck-in-the-mud
A version of the classic game of 'tag', which relies on a decent amount of space being available. One person is 'It' and has to tag the others. When someone is caught they stand with legs apart and arms outstretched until a free person manages to crawl between their legs (or duck under their arms if that is deemed more appropriate), which then 'unsticks' them.

Limit the area in which this can take place, maybe to the size of half a badminton court, and frequently change the person who is 'It'.

Tennis-ball tag
Again, space is needed (although you do not want the ball to roll too far away). One person has a tennis ball and has to hit any of the others – who are running about trying to get away – by throwing it. When someone is hit, they take over and try to get another person, and so on. Be careful of anyone nearby who is not attached to your group; being hit by a flying tennis ball tends to upset some people!

WARMING DOWN

This is frequently overlooked at the end of any sporting session, let alone climbing. We find it very tempting to go for the hardest possible routes at the very end of the session in order to get really tired out, and then just pack up and go home. Warming down (or 'cooling down') is an important part of the wall session and should take place after every visit. The idea is to ease your body gently from a state where it is prepared for extreme physical activity to one where it is more relaxed, aiming for a lower heartbeat and the removal of lactic acid that may otherwise contribute to overall muscle stiffness, particularly the following morning.

Allow about five to ten minutes for a cool down, during which time you should still be exercising but at a much

Cutting loose to move the feet efficiently

lower intensity than during peak performance. Climbing easy routes is the best approach, with gentle bouldering being just as good. Rehydration is an important part of a warm-down (as well as during activity) as you need to top up your fluid reserves which will flush impurities from your system.

During hard exercise peripheral veins dilate to increase the amount of blood that can be transmitted through them. This is particularly true of the main muscle groups used for the specific exercise, such as climbing. If you suddenly stop exercising there is a chance that more blood than is needed will still be pumped to the veins and muscle groups where it will pool, causing a lack of overall body oxygenation and resultant deposition of impurities. Warming down gradually reduces the blood flow to these extremities, making for a far more efficient and body-friendly end to your climbing session.

SOFT TISSUE INJURY

There is a chance that you will, at some time, experience a soft tissue injury, most likely to the fingers. This may be due to a poor warm-up routine, extreme leverage or exertion, some underlying injury that has previously gone unnoticed, or just pure bad luck.

If you suspect that you have incurred a soft tissue injury then **stop**! Continuing with the climb is a sure way to make things worse, and treating such an injury in its early stages gives a far better chance of early recovery.

Always seek professional medical advice for any injuries. For soft tissues, however, the advice is likely be along the following lines:

• RICE = Rest, Ice, Compression and Elevation

An anti-inflammatory medication will reduce any swelling and can help promote recovery.

A finger injury will stop you climbing for quite some time, for anything from one to six months. If you try to rush things and climb on it too early you will set yourself back further. A progression of gentle exercises designed to stimulate the damaged area and to promote strength and mobility should be gone through, and only when medical opinion deems it safe to do so should you start climbing again. Always consult a medical specialist for any injury of this type, and never try to do too much too early.

FINGER TAPING

You will notice that many climbers tape up some of their fingers when at the wall. As taping is only of use as part of a recovery programme, a glance around will reveal how many climbers appear to have been injured! Many climbers tape their fingers as a preventative, rather than curative, measure, which medical research has shown to be incorrect. Taping a finger prevents the underlying tendons from growing stronger, as your body will rely more on the strength of the tape than on tendon strength. Climbing without the tape later on may make your tendons more prone to rupture.

Taping is recommended by many medical experts to only be of benefit during the recovery stage of a tendon injury. When climbing activity increases as the injury heals the tape should be used less and less so that the body can strengthen and return to normal.

FREQUENCY OF TRAINING

There is a very sensible saying which goes something like 'You don't get stronger on your training days; you get stronger on your rest days.' This demonstrates that adequate breaks from training are important, not only to promote recovery and the resultant increase in strength and ability, but also to avoid injury. Research has shown that four days a week is about optimum for most climbers operating at a high level, as their bodies need to recover from the demands put upon them. A much higher frequency of hard training will cause deterioration of the muscular system as it does not have time for rest and repair.

If we use a climbing wall every other evening, for example, or just at weekends, we will be giving ourselves time to recover and there should be no problem. But bear that quote in mind: if you are thinking about undertaking a fierce training regime, maybe prior to a trip away, make sure that you build in about three days a week for rest and recuperation.

WARMING UP (AND DOWN)

4 TECHNIQUES FOR CLIMBING

This chapter includes a few pointers that will help you improve the way that you climb, in particular by thinking carefully about how you move on the wall and how this may be bettered. Climbing well isn't just about strength; technique is just as – if not more – important in many situations. All too often climbing lessons and sessions concentrate on the purely physical side of climbing, with little thought being given to why we move in certain ways and how our technique should be adapted to make the most of any opportunities for different climbing styles.

BALANCE

So much of any sport and movement-based activity is centred on balance, but with climbing this is an even more significant factor. So, what is balance? We all know what it is but it is hard to describe in words, so there are a few ways in which we can demonstrate how important it is for climbers.

Standing up

Sounds easy, doesn't it? But do you ever think *how* you stand up?

Try this exercise. Sit down in a chair, on a bench or even on a sandbag if at a climbing wall. Now stand up, but don't use your arms at all. Think about how you end up getting upright. You will notice that you have moved your upper body over your feet, and perhaps slightly beyond, to a suitable point of balance, and then pushed yourself upwards with your legs. Sit down and try standing up again, but this time don't move your upper body. It is either impossible or you will find that you have flipped over the back of the chair in an undignified heap!

Walking

Once again this sounds easy, but how many of us have ever considered how we do it? What do you reckon you move first when you move forwards? Your foot? A knee?

Try this exercise. Find a flat, vertical wall and place your heels, backside, shoulders and back of your head against it. Now, quite slowly (so that you can think about what is happening), take a step forwards. What moved first? You should find that it was actually your head and shoulders that moved, followed by your legs. Walking is a series of controlled over-balancing manoeuvres linked together, with your upper body dictating the speed and direction of travel and your legs being used to support everything above. Try the same exercise with your back flat against the wall, but this time consciously do not move your upper body, simply step forward with your legs. How does that feel?

Leg lift

Use the same section of vertical wall. Stand with your right side flush against the wall, with the outside of your right foot, right hip and right shoulder touching the surface. Place your left foot about 60cm out from the base of the wall. Now, without moving any part of you that is touching the wall, lift your left foot up. This will be impossible without either moving part of your upper body away from the wall or by moving your left foot next to your right one. Your left foot is supporting the weight of your body, a bit like an outrigger on a ladder or a flying buttress on a building, and lifting it will simply cause the structure (in this case you) to overbalance and fall.

Foot lift

This really demonstrates how important balance is, but in a very simple way. Stand on the floor with your feet about 60cm apart. Without moving anything above your hips, pick up one of your feet. You should find that you can't and it is stuck to the floor! Only by shifting your weight over the supporting foot will you be able to lift the other foot up. This exercise makes it clear how important your balance point is and how difficult, or even impossible, it is to climb effectively if you are out of balance.

Instructor's note

When coaching movement, I find it very useful to have the participants try out these four demonstrations of balance early on, while still on the flat. It certainly helps people understand what we mean by balance, and its importance in climbing. The main advantage of doing this on the flat is that, when on the wall, climbers will be using their arms to help themselves, thus losing focus of the importance of balance and making the ironing out of poor technique that much more difficult.

MOVING ON THE WALL

The logical progression now is to get on to the wall and traverse a distance. Choose an area that has plenty of holds for your feet and is at a fairly easy angle. As you climb, remember the results of the previous exercises and concentrate on getting your point of balance perfect before moving along. You should find that as a result you are using your leg muscles much more than before and your arms much less, and you will be bending your knees a lot as you shift your weight from one leg to the other as you make your way along. There may well be places where you can do without handholds at all, so make the most of this and keep the balance exercise going for as long as possible. Change direction every now and then to allow both sides of your body to be exercised, and for your brain to be able to remember how each move was completed with the minimum of effort.

This exercise is excellent even for experienced climbers. We often get so involved in pulling on holds and grunting our way bodily up sections of routes that we tend to forget the basics of balance, which in turn means that we may use our arms far more than we need to. Thus, keeping as much balance in our climbing movement as possible will save a lot of effort as we will use our arms less, saving them for moves or longer stretches of climbing where they become invaluable, such as on bulges and over roofs and overhangs.

CLIMBING ON MANUFACTURED HOLDS

There are many ways in which we can use our hands and feet on climbing holds, both indoors and out. Listed below are a few of the more common types of hold and feature that you will come across at a climbing wall, along with some suggested ways of dealing with them.

Crimp

These holds are very common and will occur on many routes. There are two main types of crimp: 'open' and 'closed'.

Using balance to stay stable on a hold while reaching for another

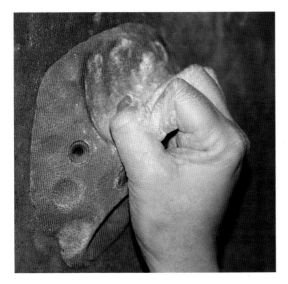

- **Closed crimp** Your fingers will be in an arched position, with your thumb brought across the top of your index finger to give support. This is a surprisingly natural position for your hand, and gives a very secure way of holding on, as long as the hold itself has a good edge.

- **Open crimp** Your fingers are a little straighter, with the tips on the hold and your thumb adding little to the overall strength. Most climbers find this less positive when being used at full stretch.

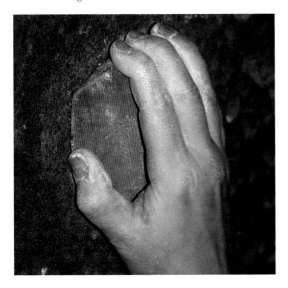

Open crimp

Note

Crimps of any type, particularly closed crimps on small holds allied with little purchase for your feet on the holds below, are very hard on your finger joints. Particularly, the tendons and pulleys that make up the structure of your fingers can come under immense strain. It is essential that you are properly warmed up before using crimps, that you have bouldered around or climbed some easy routes to warm your fingers up, and that you practise good footwork to aid support when using this type of hold. Open crimps, although feeling less secure, do exert less stress on the fingers and are a good choice until you are ready to progress onto the more demanding closed variety.

4

TECHNIQUES FOR CLIMBING

There are many types of manufactured hold where crimps are useful; almost any that offer a ledge onto which your fingers will fit can be used. Although classically a crimp will be a small hold with a flat top edge of up to 10cm long, there will be many other places where you will find that a crimp will be a better option than perhaps the more obvious ways of holding on. Crimps are also useful as side-pulls, where the hold has been mounted vertically. These can be useful when performing a layback manoeuvre (see below).

Jug

This is a generic term for any hold that is large enough to get most of your fingers around, if not your whole hand. Also known as 'thank God' holds, you would expect to find plenty of these on easier routes but far fewer on more technical climbs. Having said that, steep roofs and overhangs will often have plenty of jugs on them, as the steepness of the route more than adequately makes up for the size of the holds!

There is no specific way to use jugs. Be aware that some route setters like to use jugs at points where your hands have to 'match', using the same hold for both, so that you swap hands for the next move. Thus, if you take up all the available space on the hold with one hand, you may have trouble matching and then moving on.

Most routes will have a good-sized 'finishing hold'. These are also often known as 'finishing jugs', as they give you something large to hang on to while clipping the top anchor.

(Left) **Using an undercut**
(Right) **Using a sloper**

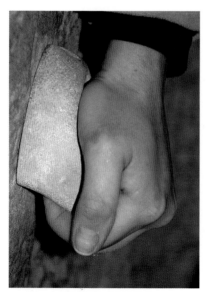

Undercut

These are very useful, and quite often overlooked. They are often jugs that have simply been mounted upside down, although an undercut could be a hold of any size. Apart from making up awkward sections of normal routes, a common place to find an undercut is below a roof section, where it needs to be used so that you can get your body well out from the wall in order to reach around the roof and get another hold.

Slopers

These tend to be quite large holds and something of an acquired taste! They do not feel particularly positive when you first come across them, but perseverance is the way ahead. The classic shape is akin to a small football cut in half and bolted to the wall, with around about the same frictional properties! Many variations exist, with some obviously providing more opportunities for progression than others. The key is often to get as much skin in contact with the hold as possible, thus increasing the amount of friction. It is also very important to have the rest of your body in a position where the hold can be used to its maximum potential. For instance, if you are trying to use a hold that is directly in front of you, there is a good chance that you will ping off. If, however, you use the same hold and drop your body position down or off to one side, you may find that you can use the hold to much greater effect.

Slopers are also good holds to use when you climb past, as you push down on them in order to maintain position or to gain height.

Tufas

These curious-looking holds are often linked together to create one long feature, and could even run for the entire height of the wall. Designed to mimic a feature found on some limestone crags, tufas can be very hard work to climb, particularly if the route setter has stated that you have to use them for both hands and feet. They are often best overcome using a mixture of layaway moves (see below) and pinches. Pinches tend to use all your hand, rather than just your fingers, around the hold; if you feel about when you first place your hand on a tufa you will find that the curves and lumps on the surface will allow you to get a reasonable grip.

They are quite tiring to climb, so every now and then it is worth taking a moment to 'shake out' (rest each arm in turn for a few moments) when you find a suitable place to do so.

Take note of any warning signs

TECHNIQUES FOR CLIMBING

Climbing a tufa using pinches

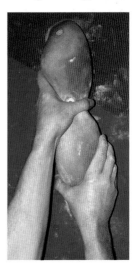

Volume

This is the slightly odd name given to large features that bolt or screw onto the wall and take up quite a bit of space, giving an otherwise featureless wall a bit of relief. They are sometimes features themselves and will usually have plenty of holes in for bolting on normal holds. Volumes are not very often used as key holds on routes for your hands, although they are very often, by default, used for the feet. If you do have to use one for your hands, often the best way is to get as much skin as possible in contact with it and rely on friction (see slopers above).

A large volume with extra holds added

MOVEMENT STYLES

Once you have gained an understanding of how some of the common holds are used, it is time to start introducing methods of using them while placing your body into different positions as you move up. Getting to grips, so to speak, with these techniques is central to efficient movement on climbing walls, and you are unlikely to progress very far without a basic understanding of how some of these common and very useful techniques are performed.

Layaway

This is a very important manoeuvre and is the key to success on many routes. It is, in essence, an 'opposition' move, where your hands are pulling one way and your feet (or foot) is pushing in the other. It is an effective way of passing a blank area of wall, or to get past a series of holds that are on a different route.

To practise the move, take the following steps:

• Find a good hold on the wall for your hands that is at about shoulder height.

• Choose a foothold not too far below it, but at a distance that you can comfortably crouch in to.

• Using the handhold, get your feet onto the lower hold and now swivel sideways, so that you are facing either left or right. The exact direction will depend on the position of your feet, how good your hands are and the direction that you need to move in.

• Arrange yourself so that, if you are facing to the right, for example, you have your left foot on the hold. Your right

foot will now need to be 'flagging'. This means that it will be out some distance in front of you, pressed against the wall to stop you pivoting off the foothold (also known as 'barn-dooring').

(Left) **Starting position for a layaway; note the foot 'flagging'** *(Right)* **Moving up to a higher hold**

- Gaining height is a combination of pulling in with your hands, pushing down on your left leg and keeping your right foot flagging. Once you can reach up, take one hand – in this case very likely the left, but not necessarily so – off the good hold and reach up for the next one. Try to keep your arms straight rather than pulling up or in with bent arms.

This all sounds very complicated, but it is a relatively simple move that is worth persevering with. Once you have got the idea and can keep yourself in the layaway position without barn-dooring, experiment with different handholds and footholds, varying the distance between them and their positioning either side of vertical. You should find that, when you are in the starting position with all your weight on your feet, there should be very little weight on your hands, making the position very comfortable and easy to rest in. This does, of course, depend to some extent on the size of the holds.

Layback
This is really a series of layaway moves linked together. It is the classic way of climbing very narrow chimneys and wide cracks, pulling with your hands and pushing with your feet. As it requires a lot of effort to complete it is quite exhausting when you first try it, but with a bit of technique it does become a bit (although not much!), easier.

- Get your hands on as good a hold as possible. The edges of laybacks will often be textured and contoured, so a moment making sure that your hand is well placed is worthwhile.

- As you move up you may wish to shuffle your hands up the holds, or to cross them over as you go. This depends on how far you have to go, how much energy you have and how good the hold is.

- Your feet are placed on the opposite wall, pushing outwards. Make the most of any holds or irregularities in the wall surface to help with purchase, as if you have to rely on friction alone you will have to keep your feet very high (not much below the level of your hands in some cases). This is obviously very tiring, and doing whatever you can to reduce the amount of effort expended will be worthwhile later on.

Friction moves
These are quite common on climbing walls, even if they only last a second or so while you swap feet on a hold. Pure friction moves, where both hands and both feet are relying on the texture of the wall surface for friction and purchase, are pleasantly rare!

Most climbing walls have some sort of texture, even if it is only a roughly painted surface. This will be sufficient for your foot to push against as you sort out the next move. Have a good hold with your hands before you step up, as this will give you more confidence. The best thing to do is to get as much boot rubber in contact with the wall as possible, which will involve dropping your heel down quite low. Maintain pressure on your foot as you make the move in order to help it 'stick' to the wall. (This is known as smearing.)

Get as much rubber in contact with the wall as possible, at the same time as pushing onto it with your toes

A good way to practise friction moves is to bottom-rope a section of wall that is a slab, laid back at an easy angle and where there are a lot of jugs to use. Try climbing the wall just using friction for your feet and any hold that you like with your hands. This exercise is very useful as it teaches you what you can get away with as far as friction moves are concerned, and it will help you to build confidence that will be invaluable when on steeper climbs elsewhere.

Some routes may need you to make friction moves with your hands. As stated above, these are pleasantly rare but can exist, particularly when bridging (see below).

Bridging

This is fairly common, particularly when climbing walls are very contoured or use corner areas as part of the route. Bridging is exactly that: making a bridge with your body so that you can either stay in balance for a moment or move on up further. Most often it will be made with your feet, with

(Left) **Bridging**
(Right) **Resting by 'bridging' a corner; note the climber is resting his arms by his side**

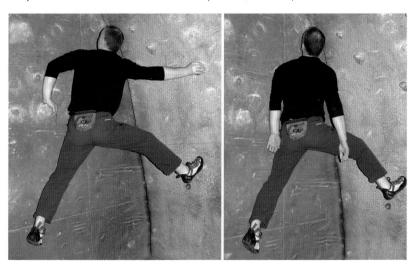

one foot on a hold on one side of a corner and the other foot on the other. However, bridging moves may also require you to move up by using friction when there are no holds available, and in this case it is helpful if you can get your feet quite wide apart.

Occasionally, you may also need to bridge with your hands as well as your feet. If there are reasonable holds available this shouldn't present a problem. However, if you are relying on friction alone for support you will have to move a little more cautiously. Maintain outwards pressure on your feet, pressing them hard onto the wall. Your hands may best be used with your arms straight and fingers pointing down so that you are using friction, similar to that mentioned above.

Dyno

Dynos, or 'dynamic movements', are the most spectacular of climbing moves as well as being those destined to cause most injuries. Dynos involve jumping from one hold to another with varying degrees of difficulty and success! The aim is to cross an area of blank wall to a hold that is some distance away by propelling your body upwards and making a grab for it once you have gained sufficient height, normally at full stretch.

(Left) **The starting position for a dyno** *(Right)* **Pushing up and reaching for the hold, timed to coincide with the dead-point**

A very important element of a dyno is the 'dead point'. This is a crucial part of the move, and getting it right makes the difference between success and failure. Imagine throwing a coin into the air. At the highest point of its path it stops for the briefest of moments before making its way

back down under the influence of gravity. The 'dead point' is the moment just before it starts coming down. If you can time your dyno so that you reach for the crucial hold at the instant that the dead point of your upward progress is reached, you will have a much higher chance of success. If you go for the hold too early you have wasted energy and will still be continuing upwards as you grasp the hold. Leave it too late and you will have started back down under the influence of gravity; grabbing for the hold at that point will not only far reduce your chances of being able to hold on to it but also will increase the likelihood of injury as your fingers try to lock on and take your weight as you accelerate towards the ground. Getting your timing of the dead point as accurate as possible is essential, and will be far easier to manage after some practice on the bouldering wall.

Dynos are often split into three categories:

- **First generation dyno** The most basic, where one hand comes off the hold that you are using lower down and makes a grab for the one that you are aiming for.
- **Second generation dyno** Both hands come off the lower hold and move up.
- **Third generation dyno** As you may suspect, both hands and both feet come off their respective holds as you launch yourself skywards!

RESTING

Being able to find a position in which you can rest is very important whether you are climbing indoors or outdoors.

On a climbing wall, rest can be gained in a manner of ways. One arm at a time can be shaken out while the other keeps a grip on a good jug. Hanging on a straight arm is less tiring than hanging on a bent one, as you will be supporting your weight with bone as opposed to having to hold it under tension with muscle. You may also find sometimes that you can hook your arm over a hold, and this will help greatly.

Bridging is an excellent way of getting a rest, particularly if you can get your feet on holds to help take your weight. In places such as corners you should find it easy to lean inwards and get completely in balance rest and shake out. This is also a good time to have a think about the route ahead.

Resting on a straight arm while shaking out, essential on harder routes

TECHNIQUES FOR CLIMBING

5 BOULDERING

Dedicated bouldering area

A number of facilities specialise solely in bouldering, and most main climbing walls have a dedicated bouldering area. It is worth noting that statistically more accidents occur during bouldering sessions than at any other time at the wall. Apart from 'normal' climbing tweaks and sprains, leaping from the top of a boulder problem onto mats and landing awkwardly can cause a variety of leg, wrist and shoulder injuries, and being underneath anyone who is bouldering is asking for trouble. Look after yourself when bouldering and climb back down your problem, at least halfway, before stepping off, and always be aware of other climbers around and above you.

WHY GO BOULDERING?

Bouldering can be viewed either as a sport in its own right or as a means to an end. The following are all valid reasons for taking part.

- As part of your warm-up regime.
- To improve stamina by climbing long traverses.
- To improve power by making short but hard and technical moves.
- To practise a variety of climbing techniques.
- To practise a specific move.
- As part of a group activity.
- Because it's **fun!**

Bouldering demands great focus and determination

As a warm-up regime

Once you have warmed up appropriately, you may well transfer to the bouldering wall for a short session. This allows you to stretch out the relevant muscle groups effectively while engaged in the activity for which they will ultimately be used.

For starters choose holds that are large and just traverse a short distance, keeping each movement very slow and concentrating on not overusing the important finger joints as well as maintaining general flexibility. Moving like a sloth is a good approach, as your body will then have time to make the most of the opportunity to get ready for harder climbing a little later on. Avoid the temptation to crank hard on small holds, at least until you are sure that your fingers and arms are properly warmed up, as you could injure yourself.

As you sense that your body is moving more freely, increase the distance that you traverse and start to vary the size of the holds. If you feel that you are getting tired or that your forearms are getting 'pumped' (a sign of lactic acid build-up), step down, shake out and rest for a few minutes. Remember that this is only part of the warm-up and you've probably got a long session with a partner on the lead wall to come!

To improve your stamina

Lactic tolerance and general overall climbing stamina can be increased by spending time traversing. You do not have to be pulling on small holds for this to be effective; just spend time traversing the wall and, when you feel tired, step down, have a rest, then repeat the process. You will probably find that on the first couple of visits to the wall you tire very quickly, but after a few sessions you will notice that you are able to stay on and traverse further as your climbing stamina increases. This becomes important if you are then going to transfer your climbing skills to long climbs, where stamina may be the key to success.

To improve your power

Some climbing moves are extremely powerful, either using small holds or awkward reaches on overhanging ground. These may involve only five or six holds until the sequence is finished, but require every ounce of your energy. Practising these moves repeatedly helps to build up your ability to produce a huge amount of energy in a short space of time, training your 'power' muscles (sometimes called 'slow twitch' muscles) to be ready to move into action. Be careful that you don't just repeat the same type of moves

Note

Take off your watch and any rings. These can get damaged and can cause injury to your hand if you slip off and they jam against a hold.

Note

It is best not to wear a harness for bouldering, as you could fall on to kit that is stored on the gear loops and hurt yourself. Remove your chalk bag when trying short sequences of very powerful moves, as you will often fall off and will puff huge amounts of chalk dust into the atmosphere.

again and again as you will build up a muscle imbalance. Vary the power moves so that you work your fingers, forearms, biceps and shoulders – as well as the rest of your body – into a state where they are 'honed' and ready to produce power on a route when needed.

Free-standing bouldering wall

To practise climbing techniques

There is no better place to practise your technique than close to the ground on big holds with a mat underneath you! You can try layaways, dynos, bridging, rests, whatever moves you like in relative safety. It is worth having a friend 'spot' you (see below), if you are trying anything 'exotic', but otherwise make the most of the chance to try all sorts of moves and sequences and see what works for you. Don't forget your feet, as good footwork as well as the point of balance are the keys to efficient climbing.

Instructor's note

Novices will often place the very end of their toe on the hold, not thinking that the inner or outer side of the foot will give them better grip and balance. Use a dab of chalk and make a mark on the inside and outside of their boots 2–4cm from the toe. They will then be encouraged to have this part in contact with the holds, stopping them from using the incorrect part of their boot.

Steep bouldering at Boulders Indoor Climbing Centre

To practise a specific move

You are leading a route, either indoors or out, on a route that you really want to nail. However, there is a particularly awkward move, perhaps a layaway from a small side-pull to a tiny crimp some distance up that you just can't get right, and you keep falling off.

Find a move on the bouldering wall that replicates the move on the route and practise it at low level until you have it cracked, then go out and finish your route off! It sounds easy, but this is a really good way to improve your overall climbing grade by adding to your knowledge of moves and sequences. At the extreme end, a few climbers operating at the very highest levels have been known to take papier-mâché moulds of holds on routes that they are failing to complete, replicate the holds in their garage or cellar, practise the moves until they get the sequence right and then go out and finish the job.

As a group activity

Bouldering is a great way to get group members both warmed up and able to understand a bit about balance, climbing holds and so on before moving on to a climbing session on the main wall. Some ideas for games and projects are given below. Make the session valuable and fun, while remembering that you don't want to tire people out too early in the session.

Because it's *fun*!

And why not? Its great fun, once you've warmed up, to have a boulder about while also having a bit of banter with your partner. Setting problems for each other to try out is not only enjoyable but also good training, working muscle groups and building up stamina and technique. On walls that have good bouldering facilities I often find that what was supposed to be a leading session ends up being predominantly bouldering, with time disappearing as you and your companion start to work out the more intricate problems and get addicted to finding ways of solving them.

SPOTTING

This is an important skill that should be used whenever the climber is in danger of slipping backwards or stumbling as they land and hurting themselves.

It would not be possible to catch them as they fall (and certainly not from any great height); the person spotting is simply providing support so that the climber does not overbalance backwards and fall awkwardly or stumble off the matting. Take up a wide stance with one leg behind

Note

Don't stack crash-mats on top of each other unless they are designed to be used that way. They are made out of a slick plastic material which is very slippery when in contact; a climber landing on top of stacked mats may find that the top one shoots away from underfoot on landing, causing them to overbalance and get injured.

BOULDERING

Tip

Many walls will set a height limit for bouldering. This is often as a safeguard for group sessions, but will also be relevant for individuals. If bouldering is allowed on the main wall a limit of, for instance, 'hands no higher than the first bolt' may be in place. Alternatively, a line drawn or taped across the wall will be the limit. This may be low down as a foot-height limit, or higher for the hands. This is set up for your own good; don't be tempted to climb high because you don't think that it applies to you.

the other, well braced. Have your arms outstretched with your hands just behind – but not touching – the climber's upper back, ready to take the weight if need be. Should the climber fall, use your braced position to guide them down in a controlled fashion to a safe landing area. Don't try to catch them or you will end up getting hurt yourself, so think about your own safety – being landed on by a flailing companion is extremely uncomfortable!

Instructor's note

If you are spotting group members, make sure that they are fully aware of what you are doing, and why. Physical contact with various parts of their body is likely if they slip off, and you need to clarify that they are happy for you to spot them in an appropriate manner as possible, so that no misunderstandings arise. When working with groups of small children who do not have their own supervising adults, choose a bouldering activity where spotting will not be necessary. In any case, there is a limit to how effective young children or those unable to give their undivided attention to spotting will be.

Spotting when bouldering

GAMES AND CHALLENGES

When working with a group there are a number of ways in which you can use bouldering as part of a session; this could also work with friends, as well as being part of a more structured session with clients. What follows are a few ideas for using bouldering in a fun way; many more exist, and half the fun is for you to find out what works for you and your companions. Helmets are recommended for all climbers, particularly for the under 18s. You may also need to set a height limit that can easily be recognised by participants when on the wall. Just saying 'one metre' won't work when everyone is getting excited.

Shark attack

Good for young folk, and can be used as part of a warm-up. Get them to trot along the bottom of the wall and when you shout 'Shark attack!' they have to leap out of the 'water' onto the wall. The last person off the ground gets 'eaten', and this continues until there is just one person left.

Clapping game

The object is for the group to find resting positions on the wall. These could be chimneys, bringing moves, shoulder jams, whatever. Give them a countdown and they have to clap their hands together as many times as possible to prove that they are in balance.

Setting a problem – 1

Great for adults. Give the group a few minutes to come up with their own boulder problem. Let them use any part of the wall to work out a sequence of moves, get the group back together again and go round to each problem. The setter can explain what has to be done and the rest of the group can try it out. To make it more interesting, after everyone has tried the problem have the setter demonstrate it in perfect style, but give him or her just one go to get it right. This will stop people setting outrageously hard moves and allow more of the group members – who can have as many goes as they wish – to succeed.

Setting a problem – 2

This time the setters are not allowed to touch the wall as they work out the problem. Once again, everyone has as many goes as they like, but the setter still has one go at the end. This method helps climbers use their understanding of how people move on the wall to work out the problem, and they will soon find that they will have to think very carefully about balance, body position, holds and distances so that

BOULDERING

Free-standing climbing boulders

the rest of the group can succeed, while still giving them a bit of a challenge.

Instructor's note

Be careful if you are using bouldering games as a warm-up for climbing routes on the main wall. Bouldering can become addictive, and by its very nature is hard work. Thus, keep this part of the session reasonably short and choose problems that are attainable and won't tire your group out before they get to the roped routes.

Enchainment
This is best done as a traverse. Start from a position on the wall with both hands and both feet on holds. Move either a hand or a foot to the next hold and then step down. The next person starts as you did, includes your hold and then adds another of their own before stepping down. Another person now gets on the wall, repeats what has gone before, and makes way for the next. Thus, each person is adding either a hand- or foothold with each go, and the rest of the group have to remember which ones they can use.

Twister
Good on walls with plenty of holds and a useful warm-up. Get the group on the wall, starting with, for instance, hands on yellow and feet on blue. Then call out commands such

as 'Left hand onto a green hold' or 'Right foot onto a feature'. It is possible to even rotate your group after a few moves so that some are facing out instead of in! Any who cannot move or who fall off are disqualified.

Pointing

This works well when working with either one or two clients who are able to stay on the wall for a period of time, and is best done as a traverse. A stick, perhaps a bamboo garden cane about 1m long, is useful. When they are on the wall point to the next holds for their hands and feet. The idea is to make it challenging but not impossible for them to climb, and they have to work out how to use the hold in relation to their body position, balance and so on. It is also good to have one client point out holds to their companion. This teaches the person on the ground which moves are possible and which are not, again making it challenging but not impossible.

Pursuit climbing

Starting on a traverse, have one climber ready to go, with a piece of material such as a hankie or sling tucked in the back of their trousers. After a few seconds, start a second climber off, who has to catch the first up and win by retrieving the cloth before the end of the wall is reached. This is useful for building up the ability to make fast decisions when climbing. Be very careful, however, that the landing is soft and that you set a sensible height limit above which they cannot go, as the last seconds of the chase tend to be quite frantic!

The freeze

All the group boulders about until you shout 'Freeze'! At that instant they must stop moving, even if they are reaching for another hold. Anyone who moves loses and has to step down. This game benefits strength, balance and endurance.

Simon says...

A good one for younger groups. This is exactly the same as you may play at home, except you are calling out holds, as in 'Simon says put your right foot on a blue hold.' Obviously, if you do not prefix the command with 'Simon says...' whoever moves is out.

The time game

A stopwatch is needed, or a second hand on a watch or clock. Starting from any point, a climber is given a period of time (this will depend on how hard the wall is, but on an easy traverse 5–10 seconds would be ample), to use or touch as many holds as possible, with the rest of the group counting. At the end of the time they get down and another person has a go, and so on. The one with the highest number of holds used or touched wins.

Three-limb traverse

This can be used at the end of a climbing session to give the group a challenge. Pair them up and stand next to the wall. Tie them together with cotton – it is essential that this is the type that snaps very easily, not a high-strength thread. Tie their adjacent limbs together, so that one person's right hand and right leg is tied to the other's left hand and left leg. They traverse the wall until one or both pieces of cotton are snapped; the next pair tries to beat that distance.

The sling thing

Tie two knots in a sling about 30cm apart and get two climbers to place the knots in their respective pockets so that they are not visible. They must then traverse the wall with the sling between them but without a knot ever coming out of their pockets.

Ninja feet

Pair the climbers up. One traverses the wall but makes every effort not to make any noise at all as they place their feet. Their partner stands about 1m away and listens for any noise. If they hear a foot scrape against the wall or bash onto a hold, the climber steps down and they swap over. This is very good for slowing people down so that they think more carefully about precise footwork and using their feet efficiently, and is an excellent way of promoting good technique with 'improver' groups.

Hoop-hop

At least two hula-hoops will be needed. The climbers traverse the wall while you hold the hoops in their way 1m or so apart. They must climb through them without touching the hoop; if they do they step down and hold the hoops for the next person. This exercise is good for stretching, layaway manoeuvres and agility.

Deportment

For this you will need a beanbag; if you don't have one wrap a sling into a loose knot and use that. Have the climber step onto the wall and then get them to traverse. They must keep the beanbag on their head; if it falls off they step down and someone else has a go. To make it more interesting, you can also include hoops as in hoop-hop above.

Football traverse

A football or a well-stuffed rucksack can be used. Working in teams of two, the group has to transport the ball from one point of the wall to another without sticking it up their jumper, dropping it and so on. This will necessitate them crossing over each other to gain position and is good training for stamina, resting positions and balance.

Dressed to climb

Get perhaps three items of clothing – a coat, hat and one glove – from each group member (this only really works with small groups), and place them on holds on the wall. The climbers then have to climb to each item of their own clothing and put it on before proceeding to the next item. The winner is the one who gets all the items on first, or is the last to fall off. This is a good exercise for balance, speed and resting positions.

Instructor's note

If you are going to be running an extensive bouldering session, in particular when focussing on technique and problem solving, it is worth having a roll of brightly coloured electrical insulating tape with you. You can use this to mark specific holds to make problem setting easier. Make sure that you won't be confusing other wall users and take all the tape off once you have finished. Check with the wall staff if it's OK to do this, as they may have their own sessions running alongside yours and not want you to mark the holds.

Well-designed and padded bouldering wall

6 TECHNICAL SKILLS

This chapter will focus on some of the technical skills needed at the climbing wall. You may only need a couple of things to get you going, but here subjects such as knots, belaying and the like are covered, all of which will probably be needed at some stage.

TYING ON

Tying on is obviously important! As the climber you need to be secured to the rope safely so that the impact of any fall is taken by the harness and your belayer.

Two knots are in common usage, the first – **rethreaded figure of eight** – being by far the more popular. This knot does indeed look like the number '8' when tied correctly, so it is easy to see if it has been done properly or not. The photographs below show how to tie the knot.

Make sure that the loop created when the knot is tied is about the same size as the abseil loop on your harness, and certainly no larger than your fist. The tail end of rope emerging from the knot should be about 30cm in length. Pull all the four sections of rope to make the knot nice and tight.

You need to secure the end of the rope with a **half a double fisherman's knot**, often just called a **stopper knot**. The function of this knot is to ensure that the main knot, the

RETHREADED FIGURE OF EIGHT

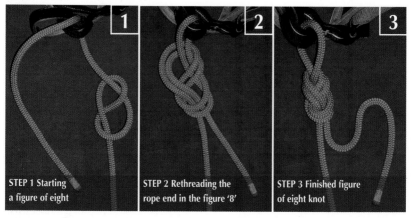

STEP 1 Starting a figure of eight

STEP 2 Rethreading the rope end in the figure '8'

STEP 3 Finished figure of eight knot

Colour and great shapes make the climbing interesting at Redpoint Climbing Centre

Instructor's note

The function of the half a double fisherman's knot, or a 'stopper' knot as it is commonly called, varies according to the tying-on method employed. If the climber is tying on to their harness with a figure of eight rewoven, all the stopper knot does is to ensure that there is sufficient tail left after completing the main knot so that it cannot unravel or the end pull through when the knot is subject to a loading. Thus, in theory, a length of rope equivalent to that needed to tie the stopper could simply be left hanging down below the figure of eight. However, I would highly advise against this for two main reasons. Firstly, if a leader is alongside an extender and clips the wrong section of rope in, it will simply pull through as they climb on, leaving them open to a long fall. Having a stopper knot in place will prevent this from happening.

Secondly, if a climber is used to leaving a long tail and then changes their tying-in method from a figure of eight to a bowline, they are opening themselves up to great danger. A stopper knot is an intrinsic part of the strength of a the bowline, as without it the knot can easily loosen, rotate and fall apart, either when loaded or simply as the climber ascends if it is not firmly tightened.

For these reasons, I would strongly recommend that you always teach the tying of a stopper knot.

HALF A DOUBLE FISHERMAN'S KNOT

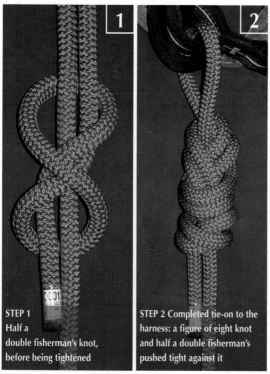

STEP 1
Half a double fisherman's knot, before being tightened

STEP 2 Completed tie-on to the harness: a figure of eight knot and half a double fisherman's pushed tight against it

figure of eight, cannot undo while you are climbing, and it is tied using the tail end of rope that emerges from the figure of eight knot. Tie it snugly to the figure of eight and practise getting the rope length right so that you end up with a short tail of about 5cm.

The second knot used for tying on is the **bowline**. This is certainly less popular than the figure of eight, but its main advantage is that it can be untied easily once subjected to a lot of loading. Thus if you are 'working' a route at the wall and are expecting to be taking a number of falls, you may decide that a bowline is the better option.

It is important that you tighten the knot by pulling evenly on both the end of

BOWLINE

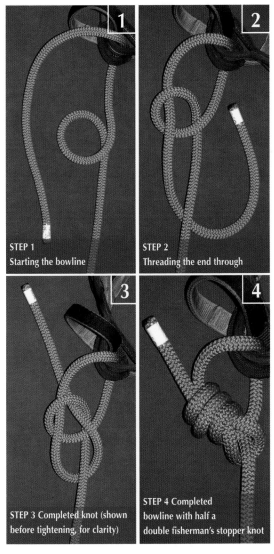

STEP 1
Starting the bowline

STEP 2
Threading the end through

STEP 3 Completed knot (shown
before tightening, for clarity)

STEP 4 Completed
bowline with half a
double fisherman's stopper knot

the rope and on the rope that is running away from you. If you do this incorrectly, you may distort the knot and end up with something that has no holding power.

Once you have tied the bowline, it is **essential** that you tie a half a double fisherman's stopper knot snugly up against it. As the bowline is basically a loose knot, the stopper is needed to secure it during use. This is tied around the loop that you have formed by tying the bowline on to your harness.

It's worth heeding
the warning signs!

**check your
knot!**

FIGURE OF EIGHT ON A BIGHT

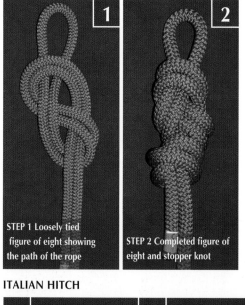

STEP 1 Loosely tied figure of eight showing the path of the rope

STEP 2 Completed figure of eight and stopper knot

ITALIAN HITCH

OTHER KNOTS

There are a few other knots that we need to consider. These will, for the most part, be used in the more technical sections, such as when an instructor needs to abseil from a high platform, but are included here for completeness.

Figure of eight on a bight

This is sometimes used to attach the climber to the rope when using a karabiner during group bottom-roping sessions. The knot looks exactly the same as for tying on to the harness detailed above, except that it is not tied around anything but just creates a free loop at the end of the rope. It is best finished off with a half a double fisherman's stopper knot.

STEP 1 Starting the Italian hitch

STEP 2 Uncross your hands

STEP 3 Put your palms together

STEP 4 Completed Italian hitch clipped in to an HMS karabiner

Italian hitch

This is useful for belaying, particularly when working with groups. It is essential that it is clipped in to an HMS karabiner, as a D-shape karabiner could cause it to jam.

Clove hitch

This is a secure knot but one that can be adjusted once it has been clipped in to a karabiner. Of little use generally, it can be used to attach clients to an anchor as a safeguard while another part of the system is readied.

Lark's foot

The main use for this is to attach the sling to your harness if you are using a ground anchor. It also has a more technical application when setting up an instructor's abseil rig. The lark's foot is quite a weak knot, reducing the strength of the

CLOVE HITCH

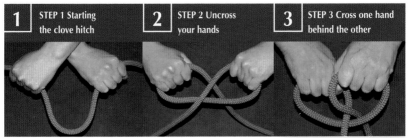

| **1** STEP 1 Starting the clove hitch | **2** STEP 2 Uncross your hands | **3** STEP 3 Cross one hand behind the other |

sling by around 50 percent, so it should never be tied in a situation where it will be shock-loaded.

French Prusik

This technical knot is used by instructors when abseiling and also when solving some emergency procedures. A loop of 6mm dynamic rope, measuring 50–55cm across once tied with a double fisherman's knot, is used. Commonly, instructors will carry two of these on their harness. This knot moves freely along the rope until it is loaded via the karabiner, whereupon it will grip the rope and lock off. Very importantly, though, it is possible to release any weight held while the knot is loaded by pulling down on the end of the coils away from the karabiner.

4 STEP 4 Completed clove hitch clipped in to an HMS karabiner

LARK'S FOOT

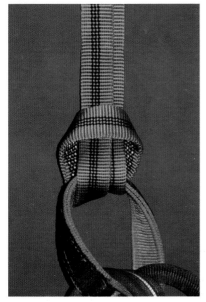

FRENCH PRUSIK

BELAYING

It is imperative that you are proficient in the use of a belay device before your companion launches themselves on to a route. Having a companion at the top of a wall and then realising that you aren't *quite* sure how to lower them effectively is asking for trouble.

Before using it on long routes, practise with your belay device at home and then on very low sections of the wall, to make sure that you are completely happy with both its operation and your ability to control it properly.

It is important to understand the difference between the 'live' rope and the 'dead' rope (particularly as they will be referred to in the following sections).

- **Live rope** The one that emerges from the front of the belay device and goes to the climber.
- **Dead rope** The one that comes out of the back of the device and which is used to control the climber's descent. **Irrespective of which belay device is being used, it is essential that that the belayer never lets go of the dead rope.**

Where the belay device is attached must also be clarified. When climbing outside on rock, best practice is for the belayer to tie on to the end of the rope and clip the belay device into the rope loop thus formed. This keeps the system dynamic all the way through. However, although there would be no problem with belaying like this indoors, most climbers will clip the belay device in to the strong sewn loop on the front of the harness (the abseil loop, sometimes called the belay loop). Avoid clipping the device in to any other part of the harness as it may not be a load-bearing part of the structure, or it might cause the karabiner to be loaded incorrectly.

Using a slick belay device on a bottom rope

Push the rope through the belay device, making sure that the dead end of the rope sits on the side that has grooves (if they are present). Clip this loop of rope and the device's retaining wire in to an HMS screwgate karabiner; clip this in to the abseil loop on your harness, and do up the screwgate. Make sure that the dead rope is coming out of the bottom of the device; if it is coming out of the top then undo it all, turn it round and reconnect it.

To take the rope in:
- Place your right-hand palm on the dead rope quite near the device and your left hand on the live rope at about head height.

Note

Always be attentive when belaying and think ahead, just as the leader is doing. Be ready to pay out rope to them when they are going for a clip. It should be obvious that this is about to happen as you can see them let go of a hold and reach down for the rope. There is nothing worse when leading than reaching for the rope on a scary clip only to find that your belayer is busy chatting to the far more interesting person belaying on the route next door!

- Pull down on the live rope and at the same time pull up on the dead rope, so that both hands move the same distance, no more than about 0.5m.
- Now bring your right hand down in front of you below the device so that the dead rope is pointing at the floor.
- Take your left hand off the live rope and put it on the dead rope just above your right hand.
- Now move your right hand to just above the left.
- Finally, move your left hand back up to the live rope at about head height, and repeat the process.

STEP 1 Starting position

Step 2 Taking in

STEP 3 Bringing the right hand down below the device

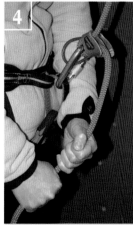

STEP 4 Left hand above right

STEP 5 Right hand above left

STEP 6 Back to the starting position

TECHNICAL SKILLS

Hand position for lowering a climber

This process may seem complicated but it will become simple to use after just a minute or two. It is important that a hand is always on the dead rope, hence swapping the hands as described. Once you have got the hang of it you will find that you can give your partner some help if necessary by taking in all of the slack rope, making it nice and snug, then standing on tiptoes and repeating the process. When you sink back down the rope between you and the climber will be nice and tight, giving a climber who is tiring or about to try a tricky move a lot more confidence.

Once your partner is at the top of the climb they will need to be **lowered back down**.

• Take the rope in tight as described above. Communicate with the climber and make sure that they are ready to be lowered.

• Move your left hand down so that it is a short distance above the right and ensure that the rope is pointing towards the floor. Gripping the rope with your left hand, move it up and towards the device (stopping about 5cm short) so that some rope is paid through.

• Now grip the rope with your right hand and feed it upwards, at the same time moving your left hand (which is no longer gripping but still around the rope) down to meet it. When they touch, your left hand grips and feeds the rope up again.

These movements are only about 30cm at a time, but this shuffling motion means that the rope is never released by either hand; both stay in contact with the dead rope, thereby providing a good deal of security. As you get used to this technique, you will increase your speed and fluidity, while maintaining control.

Using a slick belay device to belay a leader
This demands a lot of concentration and the ability to manage the rope in both taking in and paying out modes.

• Place your right hand on the dead rope about 0.5m below the device and your left on the live rope just above the device.

• As the leader ascends, move both your hands the same distance so that your left hand moves away from the device and your right hand moves towards it, feeding the rope in.

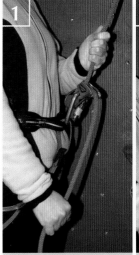

STEP 1 Starting position for paying out rope to a leader

STEP 2 Hand position having paid the rope out

Tip

Make sure that you do not get your hand any closer than about 5cm from the device when lowering, otherwise there is a chance that some skin could get caught in it (a very painful experience).

When your right hand is just below the device, loosen your grip very slightly for a split second and quickly slide your hand back down to the starting position again, then move your left hand back to its starting point and repeat the process. **It is essential that your right hand never leaves the dead rope.**

At times, the leader may need extra rope so that they can reach up and clip an extender. You will need to speed up the paying out process so that they are not literally hanging around while you pay out a few centimetres at a time. Give them plenty of rope and then take back in any extra slack once they have clipped the extender.

At times you may need to take the rope in instead of paying it out. This may be because the leader has clipped a high extender, or perhaps has down-climbed a distance and is then climbing up again. Taking in is done in the same manner as for belaying on a bottom rope (see above).

Using a self-locking belay device on a bottom rope
Although these devices are called 'self-locking', they are in no way 'hands free' (despite what you may see happening at some climbing walls!). It is essential that you hold the dead rope at all times, otherwise your partner could end up taking a very long fall.

There are a number of very good devices on the market and all will come with detailed instructions about how they should be used. We will look here at the most popular device,

6

TECHNICAL SKILLS

Tip

There is an excellent video on the Petzl website showing how to belay a leader using the Grigri. Go to: www. petzl.com/en/outdoor/ belay-devices/grigri.

the Petzl Grigri, but this is not to say that other equally effective devices should be ignored. (Note that the Grigri is designed for right-handed operation only.)

The Grigri has the correct orientation for the rope stamped on it. Swing the protective cover open and wrap the rope around the cam in the correct manner. Close the cover and clip the device to a screwgate karabiner, clip this to the abseil loop on your harness and do it up. Make sure that the device is sitting with the lever arm on the left-hand side and that there are no twists around the rope.

The internal section of a Grigri

- **Taking in** should be carried out in exactly the same way as with a slick belay device (above).
- **Lowering your partner** from the route is quite different.
- Having taken in all the slack rope, you need to orientate the dead rope over the right-hand side of the Grigri where there is a rolled edge to help with control.
- Holding this rope tight with your right hand, get hold of the lever on the left of the device with your other hand. Pulling back on this lever eventually releases the internal cam system, which lets the rope slide through. Gently pull the lever back until you have the weight of the climber with your right hand.

Lowering with a Grigri

- Now move this hand forward towards the device, letting the rope pay through it. Once you are a few centimetres away, close the cam, slide your right hand back down the dead rope again and repeat the process.
- Once you have got used to lowering in this manner, refine the technique to make the lower smoother by pulling back gently on the lever to release the rope and then control the speed of descent by adjusting the amount of grip that you exert with your other hand. Be very careful that the rope does not slide through too fast, always start slowly and keep the descent gradual and under control. The cam can be used to assist the braking motion, but it must never replace the control that you will have with your hand on the dead rope.

If you are using ropes that move quite slickly through the device, or you are finding it hard to control the lower, you could invest in a karabiner that has been designed to add

Note

The Grigri is rated for ropes of 10–11mm, but the manufacturers say that ropes of 9.7mm diameter are acceptable. However, you will find that this diameter of rope is extremely hard to control. It is so thin that holding it with your right hand and effectively lowering your partner is very tricky. Stick with ropes of 10mm and above, or change your belay device.

friction to the system. Karabiners such as the Freino have an extra section into which you clip the rope when lowering. This markedly increases the friction, thus control, which you have over the descending climber. The rope should only be clipped in for lowering purposes and not for taking in or when belaying a leader.

Freino karabiner being used with a Grigri

Using a self-locking belay device to belay a leader
When the leader is climbing at a steady rate, you should find that it is possible to pay the rope out to them by using the Grigri in the same manner as for a slick device (above). However, if the rope is thick and causes the cam to 'snatch' every so often, or if the leader needs to pull through a lot of rope quickly to clip an extender, you need to operate the Grigri differently. The instructions supplied with the Grigri include a method that allows the paying out of rope, but it also means that you have to take your hand from the dead rope. This is worrying for most people, especially if a thinner rope is being used. A second method has evolved, and is detailed here.

Tip

When using any self-locking belay device, always give the rope a test tug once the system is set up, to ensure that it is orientated correctly within the device. It is very easy to get it wrong, so a final check is always a good idea.

6

TECHNICAL SKILLS

- Belay with the palm of your right hand downwards. When rope is needed by the leader, bring this hand up (still holding the dead rope) in a curve so that you end up with your right thumb on top of the cam and your index finger underneath the curved metal section (the rope roll bar) on the right of the Grigri. The dead rope is still held by the three other fingers.

Using the roll bar to hold the device in position when paying out to a leader

- Squeezing down on the cam with your thumb, relax your grip on the dead rope ever so slightly so that you can pull some through with your left hand, as much as the leader needs. As soon as they have enough, take your thumb from the cam and put your hand securely around the dead rope again.

This method does take some practice but will become very quick and efficient to perform.

USING SELF-LOCKING BELAY DEVICES CORRECTLY

Self-locking belay devices have been associated with a number of accidents at climbing walls. This is not the fault of the devices but the manner in which they have been operated. Using them 'hands free' is one cause and is an absolute no-no. The other is called the 'panic pull'. This is where a belayer is lowering their companion only to start losing control. As they panic, they pull hard on the releasing lever, which seems like the natural thing to do. This of course releases all friction, and if control of the dead rope is lost then the climber could hit the ground. Some devices avoid this problem by having built-in safeguards or a different lowering mechanism, so be sure that you are completely happy with the operation of your device before using it on your friends!

Note

Most self-locking devices need to be shock-loaded into operation. If the climber is very light, there is a lot of friction through the extenders or they just lower themselves gently on to the rope, there is a slight chance that the cam will not be pulled into the braking position and the rope can still move freely around it. It is better to load the device quickly rather than slowly to ensure that the cam operates correctly.

Using an Italian hitch

This will normally be the technique used by an instructor who is running a group session, either as a top rope or a bottom rope on a ground anchor. It provides a good level of security and control, and has the advantage that the load is transferred directly to the anchor, with the instructor being out of the system. The mechanics for doing this are covered in Chapter 9.

DYNAMIC BELAYING AND REDUCING IMPACT

This is a technique that can help to reduce the chance of injury for someone taking a leader fall. In a very static situation, where the belayer is tied to a ground anchor and using a self-locking device on a fairly well-used, thus not very stretchy, climbing rope, the weight of the falling climber will come straight on to the system at the lowest point of the fall. As there is very little 'give' anywhere in the system, the energy created by the fall will be dissipated by a loading on the climber's body and by their mass swinging in to the wall at some speed. You can probably imagine that this is obviously more of a problem on vertical walls than on overhangs.

Dynamic belaying allows for a bit of extra 'give' in the system, thus reducing the effect on the climber's body mass at the end of the fall. This can be called the 'ABR' process, where A = anchors and the bottom, B = belayer, belay device and operation, and R = the rope.

- **A for anchors** If the belayer is not using a ground anchor (see below), they will tend to be lifted up and off the ground a little (the distance depends on the length of the lead fall and comparative weights of belayer and climber), when the leader drops. The more the upward movement of the belayer, the more the impact force (the loading on the system from the leader at the lowest point of the fall) is reduced. Tests have shown that upward movement of 1m is of the most benefit when reducing impact force. Take care if your belayer is a lot lighter than you, though, as it would be possible to pull them up and into the wall, causing injury. In that case, a loose connection to a ground anchor may be appropriate. Sandbags are very useful in these situations, because as they are mobile they will also tend to move a little once the belayer has a load applied to them (see Note under Ground anchors below).

- **B is for belayer and belay device** The belayer can help the above process by not only being ready to hold a fall but also by giving a bit of a hop as the weight of

The maximum friction with the Italian hitch is with both ropes being held parallel, the dead rope right next to the live one. The further apart they are the less the friction. Because of this, the anchor should always be a little behind the belayer, so that the ropes can be held parallel with ease.

6

TECHNICAL SKILLS

The aftermath of holding a leader fall, with the belayer well off the ground; a sandbag would have helped to reduce the distance travelled!

the leader comes on to them. This will help to reduce impact force. Another method is to use what is called 'dynamic belaying'. This is a very hard thing to do and should not be attempted except by the very experienced. This is where a little slippage is allowed through a slick belay device, thus reducing the impact force. The idea is that you have hold of the dead rope about 1m away from the device and bring this hand in quickly as the leader's weight comes on to the system. It would be very easy to lose control of the rope when performing this, as well as being extremely difficult to carry out. I would recommend that you concentrate on moving as a belayer as a first line of defence and leave dynamic belaying until you are completely happy with the belaying process.

- **R is for rope** All dynamic climbing ropes have an elongation to them, and stretch a little when loaded. This goes a long way towards protecting the climber when their weight comes on to the system as it slows them down before the full impact comes into play. It is because of this elongation that low-stretch ropes, commonly used as bottom ropes, should never be used for leading. Choosing a rope that has good elongation properties will do a lot to reduce impact force and the subsequent chance of injury if the climber swings in to the wall.

You can appreciate from the above that movement within the rope and belay system is very desirable when leading routes. In a bottom-rope situation it is not so important, as there should never be a chance of a falling climber accelerating. However, when choosing to lead have a think about the ABR and its appropriateness to the route that you are about to do.

Instructor's note

When belaying a leader, you may come across a dynamic belaying technique whereby the belayer stands some distance from the base of the wall, perhaps 4–6m out, while the leader ascends. The idea is that the forward movement of the belayer when holding a fall will introduce a dynamic braking effect into the system, thus reducing the shock-loading on the leader as the rope comes tight on him. ▶

Note

Remember that the ABR consideration is only for belaying a leader. In a bottom- or top-rope situation the rope will be snug to the climber with very little slack, thus there is little chance of them falling any distance and picking up enough speed to do themselves any damage.

TECHNICAL SKILLS

◄ However, think very carefully before teaching this technique, as it should only be taught to, or used by, very experienced climbers. It is essential that the leader has clipped the third or fourth extender before the belayer moves back, as this introduces a small amount of friction into the system, and also means that there is more rope run out, thus more rope stretch. However, the load on the belayer could still be considerable and they do have a high chance of being pulled forwards and off their feet, with possible loss of control of the dead rope. Walls that are sculpted – where the rope may be running across the surface or around a bulge – will increase the friction, thus reducing the pull on the belayer, so staying out from the base of the wall to help with the dynamic braking effect may be an option. Walls that are vertical or overhanging but smooth may introduce little friction into the system, so substantial movement of the belayer in the event of a fall would be expected.

There is a huge judgement call here, as to have less experienced belayers standing out some distance from the wall and expecting them to be able to safely belay their companion may be a step too far, certainly in the early stages of instruction. If in any doubt at all, the belayer should be close in to the base of the route. An understanding of this process can be introduced, if appropriate, when they become experienced and happy with belaying and when they can make an informed judgement for themselves on a route-by-route basis.

Sandbag being used correctly in belaying

GROUND ANCHORS

A number of walls provide ground anchors: a method of securing yourself to the ground so that you don't get pulled off your feet in the event of the climber that you are belaying putting their weight on to the rope, either in a fall or when being lowered from the top.

Obviously, if there is a weight difference (in that you as the belayer are heavier than the person climbing) this may not be an issue, but if the climber is significantly heavier than you, a ground anchor could be a good idea.

Sandbags are in common use. They are heavy enough to make a secure anchor when clipped to your harness, but just light enough so that they can be moved from the base of one climb to another. You connect them to the bottom of your abseil loop with a screwgate karabiner (often supplied), and stand in front of them to belay.

The belayer's position here is very important. You must be in front of the bag and tight on the attachment sling (which is usually sewn on to the bag and through which the karabiner is clipped). It is also important that the sling is clipped to the front of you around the correct side of your body. For instance, if you are belaying with your right hand on the dead rope, the sling from the bag must also be on your right-hand side. If it were on the left, you would be pulled round when taking the weight of the climber.

Floor anchors in the form of bolts or links recessed underfoot are also common. You would usually have to clip into these using your sling and screwgate karabiner. The note about having your belaying hand on the same side that you are clipped to the anchor (see above) is also relevant here.

Recessed floor anchor

GROUND ANCHOR PROS AND CONS

Some walls actively discourage the use of ground anchors and won't have them in the building. The argument is that although they will allow a lighter belayer to be more stable when belaying a heavier companion, poor technique could result in injury to one or both climbers. In one instance, the slack attachment of a child to a ground anchor resulted in them being pulled upwards when a fall occurred; they panicked and let go of the rope. Ground anchors can also present a hazard when someone belaying a leader steps back and trips over them. Assess the situation, the advantages or otherwise of using a ground anchor, and make a decision based on experience and, if necessary, advice from the wall staff

TECHNICAL SKILLS

BOTTOM-ROPING

Bottom-roping is the process of climbing whereby the belayer is situated at the bottom of the climbing wall, with the rope running from the belayer up to the top, through a connector (screwgate, pulley and so on – see below), and then back down to the climber. This is a very common method of controlling the rope and will probably be the way in which your first climbs at the wall are controlled.

There are many advantages to bottom-roping at a climbing wall. You are near to your companion/s for much of the time and will have a good line of sight when they are higher up the wall. Belaying is easy to carry out and to share, and you can help the climber by pointing out holds that they may have missed. If they are tiring you can give them a helping hand by sinking your weight onto the rope as you belay the rope in. Attaching novices is easy as you are right there and can help them to tie on. Finally, many climbing walls do not have access to the top of the structure, so deploying a top rope (where the belayer manages the rope from the top of the wall) is not a possibility.

Bottom-roping allows you to climb at whatever standard you like

Single-point, single-karabiner attachment

ROPE ATTACHMENTS AT THE TOP OF THE WALL

One immediately obvious feature of many climbing walls is that there are a lot of bottom ropes already in place. That's great, but it is important to know what is happening at the top and how these are attached to the wall. Whether they are connected through one or two screwgates or through a pulley will make a difference as to how you belay your partner. For instance, a rope running around one screwgate karabiner will create a lot of friction, thus the weight of the climber may be easy to hold. However, if the rope runs around a pulley there will be very little friction in the system, thus the weight of your companion will be much harder to hold. This will have an effect on the type of belay stance that you use and whether a ground anchor is appropriate or not.

The following are the commonest types of top connection, but many variations exist.

Single screwgate to one anchor
These are few and far between these days, as wall owners and manufacturers now err on the side of caution (quite rightly), and connect two anchors down to one point by use of a chain or similar linkage. However, some single-point anchors do still exist.

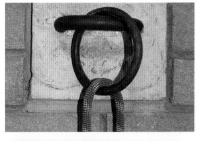

Built-in anchor
These are also a bit of a rarity on modern walls, but are commonly seen on those built during the 1970s and early 1980s. They come in a variety of types, but typically consist of a large metal staple concreted into the wall with a free-hanging ring attached, through which the rope is threaded.

Double anchor to two snapgates
Here, two anchors are linked down to one point, most often with a chain, greatly increasing the strength of the system. The rope is attached via two industrial snapgate karabiners. When leading the route, one karabiner can be clipped in to for lowering off. However, it is easy to clip both (note that the gates are facing in opposite directions for increased security), and most walls would encourage you to do this.

(Top) **Built-in anchor**
(Above) **Double anchor linked to two industrial snapgates**

Double anchor to one snapgate and one screwgate
This is a very common top anchorage rig. It gives security when bottom-roping by having a screwgate that can be done up to avoid accidental opening, plus a snapgate that can be quickly clipped in to by a leader. If that leader is then going to lower off they could just go from the single snapgate. However, if their companion is then going to bottom rope the climb the screwgate should also be used, and the gate done up, to provide maximum security. Many climbers would clip into both before lowering off anyway.

Double anchor with one snapgate and one screwgate karabiner

Double anchor to one pulley
This is also a popular system, so check to see if the facility that you are using has bottom ropes rigged like this. It will commonly be rigged in areas where only bottom-roping is carried out, and the rope will be left in place as a semi-permanent feature. The pulley reduces wear on the rope,

Climbing using an auto-belay

which is good for the centre as ropes will need replacing less frequently. However, since it also creates minimal friction at the top of the route you will feel the difference when belaying at the bottom. Be prepared for this, as you will often be pulled in and possibly up a little when your companion loads the rope. If there is much of a weight difference – with you as belayer being the lighter – consider using a ground anchor.

Auto-belays

These are a common sight at many climbing walls. Although expensive at the outset, auto-belays do away with the need for facilities to pay a number of staff to belay on different routes, as one staff member can look after a number of climbers at the same time. They are common on mobile climbing towers.

Double anchor with one pulley

An auto-belay consists of a metal casing which is attached to the top of the wall and from which emerges a high-strength webbing tape that is connected to the climber with a screwgate karabiner. As the climber ascends the device slowly and automatically winds the tape in. Should the climber fall, the internal mechanism comes into play and the climber is gently lowered to the ground, always at the same rate, irrespective of body weight.

Auto-belays do enable – from a climber's point of view – a lot of climbing to take place. For instance, someone climbing alone who wishes to train by climbing the same route a number of times (a common method) can use an auto-belay instead of having someone repeatedly take in and lower him down.

However, there are a few points that have to be taken into account. Firstly, if the auto-belay's karabiner is released when not connected to either the climber or a bolt at the bottom of the wall, the tape will fly up into the machine possibly causing damage but at the very least a delay while a member of the wall staff recovers it. It is also quite unnerving for a novice (or even an experienced climber), to commit their weight to the device when at height. As the tape is paid out as soon as there is any weight placed on it, you never have the feeling of a tight rope as you might if your companion were belaying you. It is important to practise falling off low down so that you get used to the feeling. Another problem is that, as a tight rope cannot be given, anyone who is on a hard move or becoming scared cannot be given direct assistance from below.

A final concern is also relevant to the inability to give a tight rope. There have been reports of incidents where climbers being lowered to the floor have been caught up on climbing holds. One of these was a youngster whose climbing helmet caught on a large hold as he swung round to face out, being left suspended for a moment until the helmet clasp failed. Another involved a girl whose flared trousers caught on a hold, flipping her upside down. Other examples exist.

Thus, auto-belays are a very good and versatile addition to a climbing wall and a very useful way of belaying one person at a time. However, be aware that there are a few problems associated with them and make sure that you adopt an abseil position when descending: sitting back in your harness with your feet out on the wall in front of you (see Chapter 9).

Instructor's note

There is obviously a mental risk assessment that needs to be gone through before deciding whether helmets are appropriate (the most common outcome being 'yes'), if the group needs to tuck flared trousers into socks, and whether 'hoodies' should be removed to avoid the chance of them snagging on descent.

PARTNER CHECKS

It is a very good idea to get into the habit of doing partner checks before you start climbing. This will apply to the leading section (see Chapter 8) as well as to bottom-roping. Make it part of your routine and it will soon become second nature. Just

A harness check, along with a complete partner check, is essential

before you start climbing or belaying, check that your partner is either tied in correctly or that the belay device is connected in the right way. If you are using a self-locking belay device, give the live rope a tug to check that it has all been orientated correctly. Knowing that a partner check has been carried out not only vastly reduces the chances of an incorrectly attached rope or belay device, but also helps subconsciously to relax both of you, enabling you to enjoy the climb more fully.

COMMUNICATION

Communication between belayer and climber is very important. Although the belayer should be attentive at all times and be prepared to hold a fall should the climber slip, there are a few calls that are worth remembering and putting into practice. These are not hard-and-fast rules, but are logical. You could easily make up your own sequence of calls between you and your partner, but the chances are they will be something along the following lines:

Climber	*Slack!*	The belayer is holding the rope too tight, maybe as the climber moves down a hold or two.
Climber	*Take in*	There is excess rope in the system, often because the climber has moved up a little and the belayer has been distracted.
Climber	*Watch me!*	A confidence booster for the climber (as the belayer should be watching them anyway) as the climber is about to make a tricky move.
Climber	*Tight!*	Called by the climber if they need the security of a tight rope when making a very hard move or just before falling off. The belayer can provide a tight rope by pulling in all the slack through the belay device when on tiptoe and then sinking back down again.
Climber	*Take!*	Called as the climber either falls off or rests on the rope.
Climber	*I'm there.*	Called once the climber has reached the lower-off and has clipped in to it.
Belayer	*Ready?*	Called once the belayer has have taken in all the slack, has most of the climber's weight and is ready to lower them.
Climber	*OK*	Confirmation that the climber is ready to descend.

Note that these last three calls can be changed and adapted to suit. However, some communication between the two people is needed and these are appropriate without becoming too complicated.

Instructor's note

If you are getting your group members to belay each other, you may wish to give them a formal sequence of calls so that there is no confusion over what is happening. Once all the checks have been made, the belayer can say 'climb when you are ready' to which the climber replies 'climbing' before starting to climb.

A superb wall for both bottom-roping and leading

OVERHANGING ROUTES

Bottom ropes exist on all types of routes – slabs, walls and overhangs. However, it is on the latter type of route where lowering off is a little more complicated.

Normally, on an overhanging route, the rope will be clipped in to some or all of the extenders all the way up. If none was clipped and the climber fell from the first few moves they would swing out Tarzan-like a long way from the wall, possibly colliding with other wall users, the other side of the wall, other sections of the structure and so on. If extenders are clipped though, this will limit the distance that the climber will swing.

When ascending an overhanging route with clipped extenders, you will need to unclip them before you climb past. This can be surprisingly tricky to do, especially if the rope is being held snugly.

Tip

Don't get carried away and undo the top karabiner as well – the one that is the top anchor for the rope. This has happened, so be switched on!

- First, get yourself in a suitable position for unclipping. This may be below or alongside the extender, but do not be tempted to climb to a better hold above it, as you will then be in a lead situation and it will be more difficult to do.

- The best way to get the rope out is to hold the extender with the gate facing down and make a twisting action so that the nose of the karabiner unhooks itself from the rope just in front of you. You may find that you can use your thumb or forefinger to help. It is a bit fiddly, so have a practice somewhere low down first.

When being lowered from an overhanging climb you will have to reset the extenders so that the next climber is similarly protected.

- Get your belayer to lower you down slowly and reach for the extender as it gets to waist height. Hold on to the sling section so that the outside karabiner is held pointing straight out towards you.

- With your other hand, hold the climbing rope a short distance above your harness and, pulling yourself in with the hand on the extender, push the rope forwards and into the karabiner. This is a bit of a knack but you should find that a short sharp movement will do the trick.

- Continue in the same fashion for the rest of the relevant extenders down the route.

**Unclipping an extender while
on a bottom rope**

WORKING WITH GROUPS

This section covers how to run bottom-roping sessions if
you are in charge of a group of people. These could be children, adults or a mix, the main difference between group
work and climbing with a partner being:

- The group may have little or no experience whatsoever.
- You will be dealing with more than one person at the
  same time.

Group size

The fewer people in your group the better, both for you and
for them. You will be able to give individuals much more
attention, the safety factor will be higher and each will be
able to have more goes at climbing as they will not be standing around and waiting for as long. However, from a practical (and not to mention financial) point of view, novice group
sizes tend to be at a ratio of 1:6, with 1:8 being the maximum
acceptable by many climbing walls for safety reasons.

Attaching the climber to the rope

Here you have a couple of choices: either to tie the climber in
or to clip them in with a karabiner. This choice may be made
for you by the requirements of the wall and its operating procedures, as at some walls the use of karabiners as an attachment to the harness is not allowed – check before doing so.

If you are able **to clip your clients in**, make sure that you
know the requirement of the equipment you are using. For
instance, some harness manufacturers state that two screwgate karabiners – not one – facing in opposite directions
should be used. To be safe – and if you are not sure about
the particular harness type that your group is using – go for
the two-karabiner method.

(Right) **Clipped in to a harness
with two screwgate karabiners
facing in opposite directions**

(Far right) **Single karabiner
side-loaded; this greatly
reduces its strength and must
be avoided at all costs**

A Belaymaster karabiner – the plastic closure ensures that a sideways loading is not possible

The main reason for this is that there is less of a chance of the karabiners being exposed to a sideways loading, where the weight of the climber is taken across the back bar and the gate of the karabiner. This seriously reduces the strength of the karabiner, hence the use of two. Karabiners with metal pins through them or with a plastic closure between the back bar and the gate are also available, and these have been designed to avoid the sideways loading problem. These also avoid any chance of the gate rubbing against holds, the sleeve unscrewing and becoming detached. Although this sounds unlikely, it has happened more than once.

Having said that, **tying in with the rope** is not only the best and most secure way of attaching someone but is also the technique used by climbers, and as such should be the first choice for the majority of situations.

From a group point of view a figure of eight is the best knot, as it is easy to see that it is tied correctly. Tie the initial knot on the rope, then hand the end to the climber. Describe how the end of the rope should be threaded through their harness (usually in the same line as the abseil loop), and let them thread it through themselves. You can then either take the end from them and finish the knot off, or describe to them how to complete it.

Belaying

There are a number of options for belaying a group. The final choice will depend upon a number of factors such as group size, room available, equipment available, experience of the group and so on. Some of the more common are summarised in the table and described in detail below.

BELAY SYSTEM	PROS	CONS
Instructor belaying on harness	Quick to set up, easy to provide a helpful 'tug', plenty of control, smooth, does not twist the rope.	Instructor in the system, rest of group not occupied.

BELAY SYSTEM	PROS	CONS
Group member belaying on harness	Instructor out of system, group member/s occupied, group members learning about belaying.	Time taken to teach belaying, possible panic if things not feeding in/out smoothly, ground anchor required for smaller belayers, requires group members to be sensible.
Ground anchor (usually Italian hitch)	Instructor out of system, group member can belay and thus be occupied.	Requires 100 percent guaranteed 'bombproof' anchor, difficult to provide a helpful 'tug', twists the rope.
'Bell ringing'	Instructor out of system, most/all group occupied.	Demeaning to member on floor, chance of injury to member on floor, needs space, Italian hitch not in true locked-off position.
'Choo-choo train'	Instructor out of system, most/all group occupied, rope cannot be dropped.	Coordination of group, needs a huge amount of space, decreases friction on top anchor, anti-social to other wall users.

With the exception of the first option – where a device is used on the instructor's harness exactly as it might be for when climbing with a companion – the following are examined in detail below. In order to understand which technique is appropriate for which type of client, we will assume there are two quite different groups:

- **Group A** 6 total novice 12-year-olds on a 2-hour session.

- **Group B** 4 adults wishing to learn skills for their own advancement on a 4-hour session.

Group member belaying on their harness This is a good way of introducing the group to the way that climbers actually belay. As such it is very appropriate for group B, as members can go through the process of taking in and lowering with less and less input from the instructor as the session progresses. It is also good for group A to experience, although members may find the co-ordination of taking in awkward to master. As the group is larger and the session is shorter fewer climbs may be completed. Ground anchors may be required as the effect of being pulled up slightly when holding a fall can cause a degree of panic, thus a chance that the rope will be released. It is very important with both groups that the instructor (or a well-briefed and reliable group member) 'dead-ends' the rope; the dead rope is held loosely just in case the belayer loses control when holding a fall or lowering (see Peer belaying below).

Ground anchor This is a good way to belay but relies on there being a totally solid ground anchor available. Anchors such as sandbags are not appropriate for this technique, as they are mobile once weighted. Links concreted into the floor or bolts screwed in would provide good anchors, but check with the wall staff to ensure that these are load-bearing and not just personal back-ups.

An instructor 'dead-ending' the rope coming from a novice's belay device

In the vast majority of cases an Italian hitch will be used to belay with. Also known as the 'Munter' hitch, this is a friction hitch that makes holding the weight of a climber relatively easy. It is essential that it is tied on to an HMS karabiner, as a D-shape karabiner could cause it to jam. Remember that you need to be in front of an Italian hitch for it to work correctly, so it will often be placed on a sling at hip to knee level (for details see Chapter 6).

Clients from both groups could use the Italian hitch, again with the instructor dead-ending the rope. The advantage is that, as any load goes straight to the anchor, there is little chance of the belayer panicking if they have to hold an unexpected fall.

'Bell ringing' This is definitely a technique for group A, as group B might mutiny if you tried it on them! One group member sits on the floor with their back to the wall, with an Italian hitch clipped to an HMS karabiner on their harness. The dead rope coming from there is held by one or two other group members, with the instructor dead-ending. As the climber ascends, the person on the floor holds the rope above them with both hands and pulls the slack down into the Italian hitch (hence the name of the technique). The other belayers have both hands on the dead rope and pull through the slack as it is introduced. Alternatively, the person with the Italian hitch can have one hand above and another below the knot. This can reduce the chance of unwanted slack building up if the team is not well co-ordinated.

The advantage with this technique, as outlined above, is that the group is kept busy. It is also easy to manage two routes at once, with the instructor dead-ending two ropes.

Using an Italian hitch on a ground anchor

As such it is used a great deal by groups and at climbing walls accommodating a lot of younger climbers. However, the person who is sitting down has a rough deal. For a start they are not really part of the climbing experience and are just being used as a counterweight, which may be felt to be demeaning for that individual. There is also the chance of injury, either from the climber slipping from low down and hitting them with a foot to the shoulder or head (helmets are essential), or by them being pulled upwards in the event of a fall, even a very short distance, and injuring their back on a protruding hold or featured wall surface.

Bell ringing; note that helmets are essential when using this technique for real

'Choo-choo train' I suppose calling it a 'combined group reversing belay' would also do, but I prefer my name for it... Having attached the climber, belayer number 1 is moved right next to the wall and attached to the rope coming from the top by means of an overhand knot on the bight. About 1m behind them belayer number 2 is also tied on with an overhand knot on the bight. A third belayer can also be used if necessary. As the climber ascends, the belayers walk backwards so that the rope is taken in. Once the climber reaches the top he or she sits on the rope and the belayers move back in again.

The advantages are that everyone is occupied and there are no bits of rope to let go of. However, the main disadvantage – and I'm sure you've spotted it – is the huge amount of room needed for the belayers to walk over, when (unless it is an empty gymnasium) they will be tripping over mats, bags, chairs, other climbers and so on, and generally getting in everyone else's way. Also, the further back they go the less the friction at the top of the wall. So if the climber falls off high up, or when he or she comes to be lowered, there will be quite a significant inward pull – as opposed to the normal downward pull – on the belayers. If it is a slippery surface (as is often the case with gymnasium floors) the belayers could lose their footing.

Conclusion So, which method is the best? This depends on many factors, such as the type of group, space and equipment available, so it could be none or it could be all of them (or even be a method that isn't shown here, as more do exist). Remember that safety is the prime consideration, and if getting your group to belay with you dead-ending the rope is not an option, you will probably end up belaying them yourself. For all of the many methods available, remember that climbers use a belay device on a harness, and that is often the best technique to use, demonstrate and teach.

Peer belaying

This is the term used when group members are belaying each other. Some instructors like to introduce this right from the start of the session; others may run the entire session belaying themselves. The decision largely depends on the type of group, the length of the session, and whether they are sufficiently attentive and able to be trusted to work a belay device properly and safely.

Choo-choo train

There are three main advantages to peer belaying over instructor belaying:

- **Firstly** The instructor is free to move around a little more and is out of the system, which may be of use if an incident quickly has to be dealt with quickly.

- **Secondly** (and with the right group) There could be two climbs running at the same time.

- **Thirdly** The group is learning about belaying and being involved in the whole climbing process, which is important if members wish to progress to belaying on their own.

There is a huge judgement call on the part of the instructor if they are going to let a novice belay their companion completely on their own after only a short lesson in using a belay device. For most situations the instructor (or a reliable and suitable briefed group member), will be 'dead-ending' the dead rope. This is where the novice is doing most of the belaying but the instructor has hold of the dead rope a little distance from the belayer, just in case they should lose control.

With keen and trustworthy groups it is possible for an instructor to look after two teams climbing side by side, tailing the dead rope from both belayers. This means that everyone gets more turns at climbing and more people are involved in the session in a practical way.

Instructor's note

Statistics show that the vast majority of accidents involving groups are down to instructor error, rather than mistakes by the group members themselves. In particular, lack of attention when members are belaying each other has been cited. Not dead-ending the rope, failure to check that the belay device is connected correctly and failure to check that the climber is connected correctly are the main areas that cause problems.

It could be said that one rope is the maximum that one instructor can look after safely at any time, perhaps with just two clients to work with. However, many sessions use two ropes and up to six (or even more), clients, and it is here, where the instructor is constantly being distracted by each rope in turn, that accidents happen.

Thus, be extremely careful if working with more than one rope. Running two or more is a huge judgement call based on your experience, the experience of the group and your ability to constantly monitor what is going on around you.

Instructor's note

Get into the habit of always going through a helmet and harness check with each group member before they climb or, later on, abseil. Make sure that the harness has been put on properly with any buckling system correctly adjusted, and is tight enough. Also check that the helmet is correctly fitted and adjusted and that it cannot slump over to one side of the head during climbing.

Always be very open about performing these checks, particularly with harnesses. Let the participant know what you are about to do and, when dealing with minors, ensure that any checks that you do are in full view of the rest of the group and their adult supervisor.

GROUPS WITH SPECIAL REQUIREMENTS

This is a large category, ranging from people with challenging behaviour through to those with reduced mobility. Climbing, both inside and out, is often used as a therapeutic activity, designed to challenge, engage and aid mobility for many. As such it is a good idea to be aware of a few ways of dealing with groups with particular specific requirements.

Behavioural difficulties Quite possibly the most challenging type of group members to deal with are those with behavioural difficulties, and who may not wish to be in the climbing environment in the first place. Even if they do, bravado and a fear of failing may cause them to exhibit bullish and unhelpful behaviour, very often to the discomfort of other wall users. However, once they are engaged they will very often find that their energies become channelled into physical activity, removing the need to act up in front of a crowd.

You may wish to consider whether allowing members of such groups to belay each other is a good idea or not. Very often the climbing environment will be just what they need and enjoy, so adding extra skills training such as belaying will be very well received. Be aware of what can cause a mood change, however, and avoid the trigger as well as having a plan if things start to go wrong.

Consider using areas of the climbing wall that are less frequented. This is for two reasons: firstly the group will have less opportunity to show off to other wall users and vie against each other for their attention (often one of the triggers mentioned above). Also, as some people with behavioural problems often use very strong language, it will avoid upsetting other patrons, who may complain to the wall management, with the knock-on effect of your group members not being welcomed any more. However, I usually find that as long as you don't try to patronise or be 'one up' on your group they will invariably listen to what you say (often mixed in with a hearty slice of ribbing!), and the climbing session should be as successful as any other.

Reduced mobility Groups including people with reduced mobility present a different challenge. They are likely to be extremely keen to climb, but the difficulty lies in the practicalities of actual movement on the wall.

Choosing routes that are appropriate to your group's needs is obviously very important. Slabs in particular tend to be useful as their use depends more on balance and determination than strength and agility. Slabs often also have a good selection of large holds available, making

Note

Those who exhibit extreme forms of behaviour are very often accompanied by very experienced and very skillful 'partners', whose job it is to mentor and guide their charges through the activity ahead, and through life itself. I have enormous respect for those who work with such challenging groups; watching them coax the best from their charges is a life skill indeed.

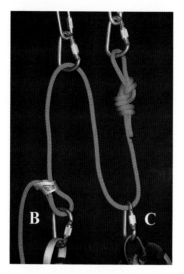

Rigged belay pulley system:
B = belayer,
C = climber

progress easier. Encouragement and not setting the final goal too high is also important. For instance, getting to the top of the wall may not be appropriate for some, but having a hold with a bit of tape around it a very short distance above the ground, to which the climber must get to and touch, will very often represent not only a huge challenge but also a huge triumph when achieved. Simply sitting back on the rope and being lowered to the ground, something probably not experienced before, will complete a fantastic climbing session.

There are a couple of methods of rigging the rope that make it possible for people with reduced mobility and grip in their arms to belay. In particular, it is possible for a person in a wheelchair to belay their friends, ensuring that everyone can be involved in the session. To rig this, you either need to have access to the top of the wall or to be able to access a reasonable distance up it safely.

The **first method** is the most practical.

- Prepare the anchor with two screwgate karabiners. Try to space these a little apart, either vertically or horizontally, as they are two separate parts of the same system and should not touch during operation.
- Tie off the end of the climbing rope to one of the screwgates with a figure of eight and a stopper knot.
- Let a long loop of rope reach down to the ground, and then clip the top side of this loop into the second screwgate. The rest of the rope runs from here and on to the ground.
- The climber is clipped on to the loop of rope with a free-running karabiner. The belayer puts their device on to the rope running to the spare coils.

Rigging the rope in this way gives a mechanical advantage to the belayer; the weight of the climber is vastly reduced when they come to be lowered, making the system very easy to control. It also means that the belayer is not subjected to an upward pull of any great degree. The only downside – apart from that it may be awkward to rig – is that the belayer has to take in more rope than with a conventional bottom-rope system. However, for many groups the advantages will outweigh any problems.

A **second method** of rigging the rope also requires access to the top anchor. The system relies on the free running of an Italian hitch at the top of the wall. Because of this, it is extremely important that the hitch is hanging in space and there is no way that it can jam when in operation. Jamming could occur if a D-shape karabiner is used instead of a large HMS, or where the hitch is pressed against the wall or some protrusion when it is loaded.

The rope runs up from the climber, through the Italian hitch and then back down to the belayer, who belays in the conventional manner. When the weight of the climber has to be held, most of it is taken by the Italian hitch at the top of the wall. The belayer will have very little effort in holding the climber's weight, particularly as the dead rope from the hitch is running through the belay device and being held at the correct angle for the Italian to provide maximum friction.

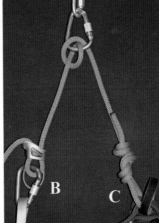

The rig for the Italian hitch top-belay. It is essential that the hitch cannot jam and that quick access to the anchor is available for the instructor

Instructor's note

Be extremely careful when choosing to use an Italian hitch that is out of reach. If it should jam at all during operation you will have real problems trying to release it. Bear in mind that you will also have a climber hanging on the rope who may have decided that they don't want to be there any more. If the climber is able to get their weight off the rope a little the Italian hitch may be coaxed to un-jam by judicious weighting and un-weighting of the system, but you shouldn't be in this situation in the first place. If you can't guarantee that the Italian hitch will run smoothly for the whole session then choose a different belay method.

Instructor's note

When working with groups who are wearing a helmet due to their age or wall requirements, wear one yourself. This may sound basic but it is important to demonstrate best practice and to set an example. Very often you will see groups with helmets on and their instructor strutting around at the bottom – or even climbing to move ropes to different top anchors – not wearing a helmet. Whether this is some type of bravado or an 'I'm the instructor so I don't need one' policy, it is very poor and gives out the wrong message. You can't insist that your group does one thing and then do another yourself.

SOLVING TECHNICAL PROBLEMS

If you are running a lot of group sessions, particularly with young novice climbers, there is a good chance that you will, one day, have a technical problem to sort out. The first – and very important – point to make in this respect is that it is really important to concentrate on *avoidance* rather than *solution*.

So how do we avoid problems?
- Choose a route that is appropriate to the group's needs.
- Carry out an accurate and informative briefing.
- Choose the correct belay method.
- Be attentive (when running the session) not only to those on the wall but also the rest of the group on the ground.
- Forward planning; use your head and be one jump ahead of everyone else.

One of the most serious problems that can occur is when someone climbs without being tied on correctly. Thankfully this is rare but it can happen, and can result in severely crippling injuries. The commonest cause is whoever is tying on getting distracted for a moment before they have finished, perhaps because their partner has asked a question or they have stopped to talk to someone. **It is absolutely essential that you make it clear to climbers that they must never let anyone or anything distract them from the moment they start tying on until they have completely finished.**

Solving the nightmare problem of a climber who is some distance from the ground and finds that they have come undone from the rope is desperately hard. The obvious answer is for them to down-climb, and hopefully this will be possible. If not, things are a good deal more serious. There would not usually be time to effect a rescue by having a competent person safely climb up to them (unless the route that the climber is on is very easy) as the stuck climber would most likely have fallen off by then. If the stuck climber is near an extender they may have the chance to clip it into their abseil loop, but this would probably mean moving up or down a bit and would certainly involve taking a hand off to clip in, not something that a petrified person would be able to do easily.

At many climbing walls the answer is to have a crash mat readily to hand in case something like this happens. There will often be a mat below the bouldering wall that you can drag across, but some venues have mats strategically placed for just such an eventuality. There are obviously questions about the accuracy with which they are placed below the stricken climber, as to be a metre or so

Notice on a crash mat, ready for use in an emergency

one way or the other would make it likely that they would miss the mat if they fell off. There is also the question of at what height the climber would be protected by the cushioning effect of the mat. However, placing a mat or two may well be the only way to solve this predicament. The best thing to do is to avoid it happening in the first place.

SOME COMMON CLIMBING PROBLEMS

The following table shows just a few of the more common problems that you may come across. The final column shows that all these could have been avoided even before the climber started up.

PROBLEM	CAUSE	REMEDY
Equipment fitting issues	Incorrect fitting session, incorrect equipment available	Proper fitting session, with ongoing checks throughout the session.
Climbing too fast	Peer belaying not efficient, lack of observation from instructor, incorrect belay device for rope diameter.	Climber told to slow down, climbers briefed to keep to speed of belayer, observation, correct belay device selection.
Climbing off route	Direct route too hard, lack of observation, poor briefing.	Choose appropriate route grade, observation, briefing, use of coloured holds, tight rope if extreme.
Climber pulling up on rope	Route too hard, poor briefing, lack of observation.	Choose appropriate route grade, observation, briefing, down-climb so that slack can be taken in.
Clothing or body part caught in belay device when lowering	Poor hand position, loose hair or clothing, lack of observation, lowering too fast.	Lowering practice, observation of loose items by instructor before session, un-weighting rope by climber returning to wall or instructor pulling on rope.

Practising a lower at the base of the wall

PROBLEM	CAUSE	REMEDY
Belayer sustains rope burn when lowering	Poor technique, belayer getting 'carried away', rope/belay device incompatible, no one dead-ending the rope.	Lowering practice, belayer told to slow down, correct choice of equipment, instructor or peer dead-ending the rope.
Refusing to be lowered from part way up/top of route	Fear, reluctance to relinquish good holds, lack of trust in belayer/s.	Practise lower at base of route, tight rope, coaxing, down-climbing, rope tricks.

Probably the most common problem that occurs is where a climber refuses to commit their weight to the rope to be lowered down to the ground once they have completed the route. This is often because the height is such that they are convinced that they will fall to the ground; and since the rope is a little stretchy they don't want to commit their weight to it. It's no good realising that a climber is nervous about being lowered from the top of the wall when they have just arrived there!

The best way to avoid this problem is to practise the lower with each climber at the start of the session, right at the base of the route. Have them climb up about 2m, then take in as much slack and rope stretch as you can. Get them to sit back in their harness in the lowering position: feet apart, legs straight, holding on to the knot in front of them, and then lower them back to the ground. If they are happy to do this with no prompting let them climb the route. However, if they are very tentative at this stage let them practise once or twice more until they are happy to sit back and let the rope take their weight.

ESCAPING AND RESCUE TECHNIQUES

Escaping the system
When preparing to sort out a technical emergency, you will need to be hands free. This process is known as 'escaping the system' and there are a couple of ways of doing it. Bear in mind that it is unlikely for the rope to be loaded during this process, as if it were loaded you could simply lower the climber to the ground. If you have taken in all the slack and stretch while trying to convince them to come down, slacken the rope off just a little for the comfort of everyone.

The first escaping method uses another group member (or a convenient ground anchor). We will assume that you are using a standard slick belay device.

- While still carefully holding the dead rope, tie a clove hitch in it and clip this to a screwgate karabiner on the abseil loop of the other group member.
- Have them stand behind you so that the rope is held in the correct position to keep the belay device locked off.
- You can now let go of the dead rope.

The second escaping method assumes that there is no one around that you can use as an anchor and no suitable ground anchor. In this case you will have to lock off the belay device around its karabiner. The knots are called a

Escaping the system using a group member

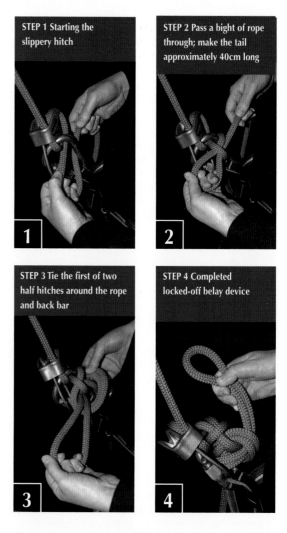

STEP 1 Starting the slippery hitch

1

STEP 2 Pass a bight of rope through; make the tail approximately 40cm long

2

STEP 3 Tie the first of two half hitches around the rope and back bar

3

STEP 4 Completed locked-off belay device

4

slippery hitch and two half hitches, and they lock off the belay device very securely. These are exactly the same as those used for locking off an Italian hitch (see Chapter 6), except that they are tied around the back bar of the karabiner. Make sure that you have full control over the dead rope until the first half hitch has been tied.

A slab rescue

There is a chance that – with the best will in the world and even after having practised a lower at the bottom of a route – one day one of your group will refuse to be lowered. This is not uncommon with novices and will most likely happen on climbs that are slabs, leaning back a little from the vertical.

There are two reasons for this. Firstly, you will usually choose a slab as the first-ever route for your novices, as it will be nice and easy with a good selection of big holds. But the whole climbing experience is new and very scary, so if someone is going to become frightened this will often be where it will happen. Secondly, group members will rarely become stuck on vertical walls and overhangs as:

- They will have progressed through the slab phase and so be trustful of the system.
- It is usually too hard to hold on for very long at the top of a steep route!

Because of this, we will concentrate here on slabs. Don't forget that talking to the stuck person is a good way to instil trust and encourage him to be lowered off. Taking in as much slack as possible and getting the stretch out of the rope by taking in when on tiptoe and then sinking down, repeated a few times, can also help. If this still isn't working, see if they will climb back down, as this will often be far quicker than performing some rope tricks. If that is no good, then rope tricks it is! **This technique therefore describes how to climb, rescue and bring down the stuck climber in a secure manner.**

- Having escaped the system, use a Prusik loop to tie a French Prusik around the climbing rope just above the belay device. The number of turns will depend on a number of factors, such as the thickness of the rope, how new and shiny it is, and so on, but it will probably need four or five wraps.

French Prusik on the rope above a belay device

- Clip a screwgate into the Prusik and then clip this into your abseil loop. If it won't reach you can clip it into the karabiner holding the belay device. It is only acceptable to clip metal to metal in this manner in an emergency situation.

- Once it is in place, push the French Prusik firmly up the climbing rope as far as it will go so that it grips.

- Now use a sling, or even a spare Prusik loop, and lark's foot or clip this to your abseil loop below the karabiner already there. This will be used to attach the stuck climber to you, so the distance between the two of you should be about 0.5m. If you are using a sling – usually the most convenient – tie an overhand knot in it the appropriate distance away from you. This is known as a '**cow's tail**'.

- A screwgate karabiner is now clipped in to the sling, which is then clipped to a suitable part of your harness out of the way. Any spare end of sling should be tucked into your waist belt or a gear loop so that you don't trip over it.

- You now need to regain control of the dead rope, so unclip the clove hitch to the spare person or ground anchor, or unlock the locked-off device at your harness. **It is imperative that from here on that you do not let go of the dead rope.**

- Now start to climb up towards the stuck person. As you do so, pull all the slack through the belay device by pulling on the dead rope. The Prusik will travel down the rope and touch the belay device, releasing its grip and allowing the rope to move. Carefully manage the dead rope as you ascend, taking care to never let any slack into the system or to let go of it.

The function of the Prusik is as a back-up should you slip backwards a little. In this case it will travel back up the rope and lock off, holding your weight as it does so. Note that this locking-off property cannot be guaranteed, and it is only there as an extra safeguard; all the work is done by you pulling on the dead rope. Also note that a Prusik that is shock-loaded – which would happen if you were to slip back any distance – may completely fail to grip, so be very careful to prevent this from happening.

Instructor's note

Instead of tying knots along the rope, you may elect to use a clove hitch method. Clip an HMS karabiner to your abseil loop and put a clove hitch onto this, tied on the dead rope underneath the belay device. Any slack rope can be pulled through this after every couple of metres.

- Every metre or two you **must** tie an overhand knot on the bight in the rope below your device: an extra safeguard in case you slip and the Prusik fails to hold you. At least with the overhand knots in place you will not be able to fall all the way to the ground. This is sometimes referred to as 'tying in short'.

- Once you arrive at the stuck climber, get alongside and make yourself safe by taking a few wraps of the dead

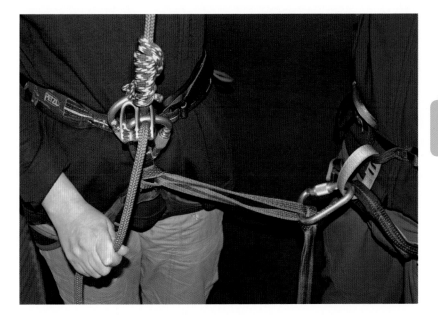

rope around your thigh, or by tying an overhand knot very close to the belay device. If the clove hitch method has been used (see box), then make sure that there is little slack between it and the belay device.

The instructor and climber linked with a cow's tail (see Chapter 9)

• Clip your cow's tail to their abseil loop and ease them back into the lowering position with you alongside.

• Remove the thigh wraps or nearest overhand knot (or release the rope through the clove hitch for a few metres), and pull down on the French Prusik to release it.

• You will now be in an abseil position, with one hand holding the Prusik released and the other controlling your descent with the dead rope. Due to the friction in the system, when abseiling you will end up lower than the climber, with the sling between the two of you snug. Your weight pulling down on this sling will pull the climber after you, suspended as they are by the climbing rope. As you pay out rope to descend, it also runs up through the top anchor and down to the climber, who will then descend with you.

• Make sure that you take out the rest of the overhand knots a metre or so before you reach them. If using the clove hitch method, pull slack through at regular intervals, well before the clove hitch gets near to the belay device.

Instructor's note

It is important that there is as little distance as possible between the front of the belay device and the start of the Prusik. Prusiks do not tolerate being shock-loaded. Thus, if there was much distance between the device and the Prusik and you slipped when climbing up and loaded it, there is a chance that it would not grip; the Prusik could melt through as it slid down the rope (this could occur with a distance as little as 1m). The other possibility is that the Prusik grips but strips the sheath of the climbing rope as your weight comes on to it with a bang. Never shock-load a Prusik and keep that distance short.

Although this technique is probably the most efficient in this situation (allowing for the fact that there is no way that the stuck person is going to move without you going to get them), there are a few drawbacks:

- You are reliant upon the Prusik gripping as a safeguard, which cannot be guaranteed.

- Your weight will be counterbalanced by that of the climber if you load the system. If they are much lighter than you, they may be pulled upwards some distance, or at least be in for an uncomfortable few minutes.

- Making your way up anything other than an easy angled slab with plenty of large holds is very tricky, particularly as you must never let go of the dead rope or be in a position where you have introduced slack in the rope above you.

- Depending on your group there may be group-management issues; while you are busy with the stuck person the rest of your group will be unattended.

Having said all of that, it does work in quite a number of situations and is a useful skill to have at your disposal.

If you are belaying using a Grigri or a similar device, you will not need to use a Prusik as a back-up. However, be aware that many of these devices require a 'jerk' for them to operate correctly, thus care must be taken if you are doing a slab rescue. If you carefully lower your weight onto the device the cam may not operate correctly with the obvious result of the device failing to grip the rope. It is essential

Note

It is as awkward having too many wraps of the Prusik as too few. If there are not enough the Prusik will not hold; too many and it will grip the rope so tightly that it becomes impossible to pull any slack through as you go up.

that you do not forget to tie the overhand knots, mentioned above, at regular intervals as you ascend.

Transferring from one belayer to another

You may be in a situation where you are out of the system and have a group member belaying their companion, who subsequently becomes frozen to the top of the wall. Obviously you cannot send them up to perform the rescue, so you need to take control of the belay device. This can be quickly and simply carried out by doing the following:

Swapping belayers by clipping the instructor's screwgate behind the belay device

- Make sure that the dead rope is being held in the locked-off position, and set the belayer up in an escaping the system mode as detailed above.

- Have an HMS karabiner connected to your abseil loop.

- Get next to the belayer and clip your karabiner through the rope at the back of the belay device. This will be right next to their karabiner and will be possible as the rope will not be loaded at this point.

- Having done up your screwgate, unscrew their karabiner and slip it out of the rope loop at the back of the belay device.

- You will now be in a situation to start setting up the Prusik for the slab rescue.

Overhanging leading on an outdoor competition wall

8 LEADING

At some stage you will want to start leading routes at the wall. This is a huge step, as both climber and belayer will have to approach the climb differently from when bottom-roping. You will no longer have the constant reassurance of a rope above you but will be completely on your own, out on the wall above an extender. 'Mind games' come into play, and you will find that you are reluctant to make moves that you could easily complete on a bottom rope. It is being able to overcome these concerns, concentrating purely on the climbing and efficient clipping of the protection, that will make a huge difference to how relaxed you are and how well you can adapt to being a leader.

BELAYING

As a leader, it is essential to have a belayer you know you can trust. Knowing that even if you fall from above an extender you will be fine, and that your belayer is always paying attention to you, will make a massive difference to how you climb.

The method of paying out rope to a leader is covered in Chapter 6. However, one of the main skills of a belayer is to be observant and be able to predict how the leader will want the rope to run. For instance, seeing the leader reach down for the rope tells you that they are about to make a clip. Once they have done this and started to move up, you will probably have to take the rope in as they get to the extender, and then start to pay it out as they move past. This all calls for a good, practised belaying technique; tricky at the start, but much easier with time.

The position that you adopt in relation to the climb is important. Think about where you would be best placed in relation to the line of extenders and make sure that the rope, particularly after the first extender has been clipped, will not become a hazard if the climber falls off. If you are standing a little way out from the wall and there is a fall, the climber could end up straddling the rope or at least running a leg down it, as the rope would be under tension due to their body weight. Plan ahead and, if necessary, be prepared to move. Perhaps one side of the route is an appropriate place to belay from as the climber starts, but as they get up a little

> ## Tip
>
> Think about using ground anchors if there is a chance that you will be pulled up off your feet and towards the wall. Dynamic belaying (see Chapter 6) is important – but so too is your safety.

higher you can move across to the other side if more appropriate. (Obviously a solid ground anchor would make this impossible.)

On steep routes, avoid the temptation to move further from the base as the climber gets higher so that you can have a better view. In this situation the rope from you to the first extender would not be going upwards but more in an outwards direction, pulling you in to the wall if you

Belaying out from the base of a route means that the rope will pull you in if you have to hold the climber's weight

Belaying on an overhanging route

Managing the rope at the start of a route

had to hold the climber's weight. Staying close in makes it much easier to control a fall and any subsequent lower.

The same applies on overhanging routes: the further out you move in order to see, the more inwards will be the loading on you in the event of a fall. A good place to be on such routes is by the base of the wall facing out, not in. This allows you to watch the climber and belay effectively, as well as not being pulled sideways should they slip.

Keep everything tidy. Have the rope neatly arranged on your dead-rope-hand side, nicely run through so that the rope to the leader's end is coming out from the top of the pile. Avoid the temptation, when changing routes, to simply drag the rope across the floor. Apart from possibly damaging the rope, it will almost certainly end up with kinks and knots, tricky to undo when you are busy belaying. In this situation a rope bag with a built-in mat is very useful, as the rope can easily be transported from route to route without any chance of becoming badly twisted.

Give the leader plenty of rope as they start climbing, holding it out of their way as they get to the first extender. When this is clipped, take the rope in and start belaying as normal.

It is very helpful if the belayer 'spots' the climber en route to clipping the first extender (see Chapter 5). The belayer takes up position behind the leader so that they can field them onto the ground should they slip during the first few moves.

Instructor's note

You may need to explain why we belay off the abseil loop indoors, but outdoors encourage climbers to tie in and only belay from the rope loop. The difference is that indoors you would expect to have bolts every metre or so, thus the loading on the belay device and abseil loop would not be very high in the event of a leader fall. On rock, however, runners may be a few metres apart or even have the chance of failing. Thus, the loading from a leader fall will be far more severe. This is why outside we tie in and then belay from the rope loop, as it is a dynamic part of the system.

CLIPPING IN SITU EXTENDERS

Many climbing walls will have the extenders (quick-draws) already in place at strategic points up the route. You should clip into all of these as you ascend; the conditions of use at many centres will state that all protection *must* be clipped in to when leading. Realistically, it would be daft not to.

Clipping position

When clipping, think about your body position in relation to the extender and the amount of rope that you have run out from the belayer. This is particularly important when clipping the second and even third extenders, as to miss the clip and fall could result in you hitting the floor.

As far as the first extender is concerned, if you miss the clip you will head towards the floor anyway, hopefully while being spotted by your belayer. However, your position in relation to the second and third extenders is very important. If you reach up high to clip it with a loop of rope in your hand, miss the clip and slip off, you will very likely have pulled through enough rope to allow you to sail down below the first runner and hit the deck. On the other hand, if you climb a little higher so that your waist is about level

with the runner and miss the clip and subsequently fall off, you will have far less rope paid out to you, thus your fall distance will be reduced and you will be held by the first (or second) runner, avoiding the floor altogether.

It may well be that you are perfectly balanced and have good holds for your hands and feet when clipping the second runner from below, so that will be fine. However, if the route is tricky and just about at your limit, think about getting close to the extender to reduce the possible fall distance.

After the third extender it is not quite so critical how far below the subsequent runners you stop to clip, although being close to them will still greatly reduce the distance that you drop if you slip before successfully clipping the rope in.

(Left) **Pulling up a lot of slack rope to the second runner, giving a chance of hitting the ground if you fail to make the clip**

(Right) **Clipping in close to the extender, and a lot safer**

(Below) **Second bolt extended for a novice**

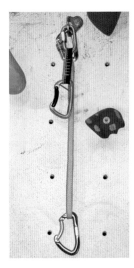

Instructor's note

When teaching leading, be very aware of the distance between the first and second extender and the chance of a subsequent ground fall. If this is a concern, clip a long extender or short sling to the second bolt. This allows the novice to lead up the lower section of wall without any chance of hitting the ground, from whatever position the clip is made.

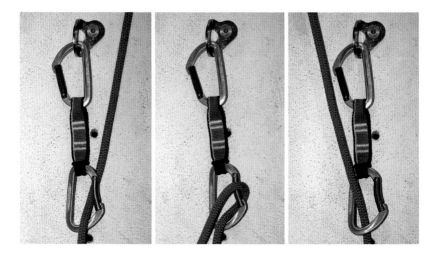

(Left) **Extender 'back-clipped'**
(Centre) **Rope running across the gate in the event of a fall**
(Right) **Extender clipped in the correct manner; karabiner is not twisted**

Clipping extenders the correct way

This is very important and, if done incorrectly, is called 'back-clipping'. As you climb, it is important that the rope runs up and through each of the extenders in a straight line, allowing the attached karabiners to hang flat and not twisted. If an extender is back-clipped, the karabiner at the end of the extender will rotate as you move up and past it. The concern here is that, should you fall off, you may have placed the karabiner so that the rope runs across the gate as you fly past, with the possibility of it opening and releasing the rope. This problem becomes more acute where bent gate karabiners are used, which tend to be in the majority with *in situ* gear.

Make sure that, as you clip the extender, the rope runs up from the belayer, behind the karabiner, through from the back and out at the front, then to your harness. As you continue on and up the karabiner will sit in the correct orientation.

Instructor's note

Extending the second runner on a climb so that the chance of a ground fall is negated has been covered earlier. When teaching a novice how to lead – particularly if they are nervous or the runners are some distance apart – you may wish to extend all the runners, not just the second one. This will nearly double the amount of points for the climber to clip in to, giving a higher degree of overall safety, more of a feeling of security and the chance to practise clipping into extenders many times.

Rigging the route can be done beforehand, with you being belayed by them or another staff member. Make sure that the extended runners are clipped in to the bolt hangers behind the existing ones, otherwise there is a chance of them becoming wrapped around one another.

Holding the karabiner to clip it

Clipping the rope in to an extender can be a fiddly process, particularly when you are 'pumped' and some way above the ground! Free-hanging extenders are particularly tricky to clip, especially if you knock one before managing to grab it, which sends it swinging. There are a number of methods by which you can make clipping a bit easier, and the one described here suits most situations. Get the hang of this one before trying any others.

- When you are ready to clip, hold the rope between your thumb and forefinger with the rope running towards your harness.

- Your middle finger is now used to steady the extender by placing it at the bottom of the karabiner into which the rope is going to be clipped. Exert a small amount of pressure and the extender will not wobble about.

- Now bring the fingers holding the rope up to the gate and press it in with your thumb.

STEP 1 Holding the rope and karabiner steady

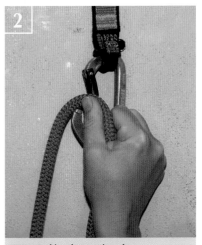

STEP 2 Pushing the rope into the karabiner with the thumb

Clipping with the 'wrong' hand in order to have a rest

Clipping when tired

It can be particularly difficult to clip an extender when you are feeling tired or a bit pumped. One answer is to down-climb a little to the last really good hold or resting place and shake out your arms one at a time, allowing you to recover sufficiently so that you can re-ascend and make the clip. While doing this, make the most of the chance to look ahead and plan out the route, making note of the line that the holds take on the way to the top chain.

The other option is to stay at the point from where you want to make the clip, but to change hands before doing so. For instance, if you have a good hold with your left hand but this is the arm that is particularly tired, put your right hand onto the hold and make the clip with your left. This will often mean reaching across your body on the inside, which changes your position and can provide some respite from the 'normal' climbing position. Once you have made the clip, revert to the correct hand on the appropriate hold and either continue or spend a few moments there, swapping hands and shaking out as appropriate.

BE WARNED...

Some climbers feel that, if you need to pull up a lot of rope to make a clip, it is handy to hold the first pull of the rope between your teeth while moving your hand down for the second pull. Don't make a habit of it and avoid the temptation to keep the rope between your teeth if you find that you have to make a move or an adjustment on the holds to make the clip properly. For instance, you have pulled up a section of rope and have it between your teeth, but realise that you have to move up a hold to reach the clip efficiently. If you make this move with the rope still in your mouth and then slip or a hold rotates, you will be falling a very long way! It is far better to drop the rope so that your belayer can take it in, reposition yourself and start again. Also, the reaction of the human body is to clench various parts when falling. Falling any distance at all with the rope firmly clenched between your teeth will result in you either losing or breaking them.

Stepping through

This can lead to a fall becoming a serious incident, and is an issue when moving above the last clipped extender. It is where the leader places their foot between the rope and the climbing wall in order to reach a hold, and subsequently slips off. As their foot is inside the rope, their leg will catch on the extender on the way past and they will be flipped upside down, possibly injuring their back or head, particularly if a helmet is not being worn. Take care always to have your foot on the outside of the rope if reaching across its line to get to another hold.

Your belayer will often be in a good position to notice this and give you a warning. Climbers often get so involved that making little mistakes are easy, but this is a little mistake that has quite severe consequences. If you are belaying and notice the leader doing this, call out and let them know.

Z-clipping

This only occurs where protection is closely spaced, and can easily happen on a climbing wall. It is often caused by a leader not thinking carefully about which section of rope they are pulling up (often because they are hanging on for dear life and wants to make a quick clip!). Unfortunately, Z-clipping means that they have exactly the same amount of exposure after the clip as they had before.

(Left) **Stepping through, where a fall will cause the climber to flip upside down**
(Right) **Stepping on the outside of the rope, the safest option**

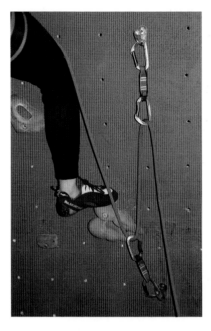

In the photograph left the climber has reached down for the rope and pulled up a length from underneath the previous extender (instead of above it) and clipped it in. This means that the rope runs from the belayer, up to the extender just clipped, down to the previous one and then back up to the leader. If the leader climbs on, there will not only be a lot of rope drag but there will be a danger of a long fall.

Often the belayer will be in a good position to spot this and should shout out if necessary. To remedy the situation, the leader should unclip the rope from the lower of the two extenders, clipping it back in to the correct section of rope once the belayer has taken in any slack.

Prevention is better than cure, so get in the habit of holding your rope right next to your harness and then sliding your hand down before pulling slack through.

Z-clipped rope

USING LEADER-PLACED EXTENDERS

Some walls offer the opportunity to clip your own extenders into pre-placed bolt hangers. Always check with the wall staff before doing this, as the hangers may be there for a different reason. Also, there may be insurance issues or other elements of health and safety. For instance, some walls will want to rope off the area below the route to be led, in case the leader drops an extender onto another climber. Obviously, walls are loath to rope off areas below routes if the place is busy, as it will stop others from climbing there.

The extenders used will be essentially the same as those already supplied *in situ* on the wall, usually consisting of a straight gate karabiner at one end, a short sling of 10–15cm, and a bent gate karabiner at the far end. It is very important that only the straight gate karabiner is clipped in to the bolt and the bent gate used at the rope end. If clipped the other way around, with the bent gate on the bolt hanger, it could, in some circumstances, unclip itself due to the ease with which the gate opens when pressed against a solid object such as the metal eye of the hanger.

Decide how many bolts need to be clipped on your route, and add an extra couple of extenders. Rack them on your harness, a few either side, and off you go. When you get close to the hanger select an extender, take it off your harness and clip it in to the bolt (ensuring that it is the straight gate). The height from which you do this does

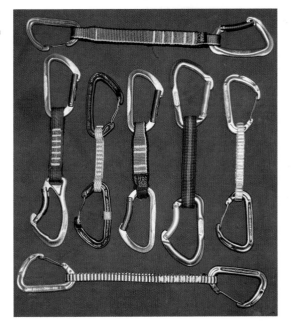

not matter a great deal, as it is when you clip the rope in that your positioning becomes more important (see Clipping position above). Take a moment or two to think about the way that the route runs after the bolt. If it heads off to the left, clip the bolt so that the karabiner holding the rope opens to the right. This will help to minimise any chance of the rope running across the gate and unclipping in the event of a fall. It is essential that you avoid back-clipping the karabiner, for reasons given above.

Once you have completed the route and are being lowered off, you will need to remove all your extenders. Have your belayer stop you level with each of them so that you

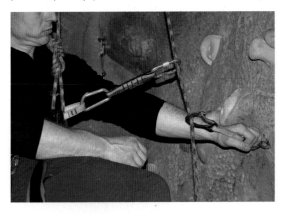

Leader using an extender to help guide him in to the wall when retrieving gear

can unclip and retrieve them, placing them back on your harness gear loops.

If you are being lowered from an overhanging route, you will find yourself further and further from the wall the more you descend. To help you get in close to the extenders to retrieve them, clip a free-running extender between your harness and the climbing rope. This will let you maintain contact with the rope and help you pull yourself inwards at each bolt.

Be aware – when lowering from overhanging routes – that when you unclip the last extender you may end up swinging some considerable distance out from the wall when you put your weight on the rope, maybe taking your belayer with you. Be very careful that you are not going to crash into the wall on the other side of the room, or into other wall users, part of the building and so on. If this is a concern, leave the bottom extender in place, lower to the ground, untie and boulder up to it, spotted by your belayer. The chances are that this placement is not very high off the ground, so this will usually be the best remedy.

KEEP AN EYE ON YOUR KARABINERS

Bolt hangers are made from quite thin metal, thus the edges that are in contact with your extender will not be smooth. After some use – and particularly after a few falls or lowers – there is a chance that the inside radius of the karabiner could become nicked and burred, with the consequence that the rope may get damaged if it is later clipped into that same karabiner. Therefore it is important that the same karabiner on each extender is used exclusively on the bolt end and that the one that has the rope clipped into it is never clipped into a bolt. If you are using a bent and straight gate rig which karabiner is which will be obvious. If you are using two similar karabiners avoid getting them mixed up by wrapping some tape around the one that goes into the bolt. This karabiner should then be used exclusively for the bolt, and can be racked on your harness accordingly.

USING LEADER-PLACED PROTECTION

Some walls offer the chance of placing conventional climbing protection, such as wires, chock, slings and cams, on the lead. The areas where these runners are placed must be the correct designated positions as they will have been made to take the forces exerted on the gear by a falling leader.

The technique of placing protection when on the lead is beyond the scope of this book (*Rock Climbing*, by the same author and published by Cicerone Press, covers these skills in detail), but suffice to say that these are not skills that can be practised by a novice. Great care and judgement are needed to place protection correctly and safely, far above that required when just clipping *in situ* extenders. Take great care if choosing to do this, and make sure that you have the correct equipment, experience and ability on the chosen grade of route.

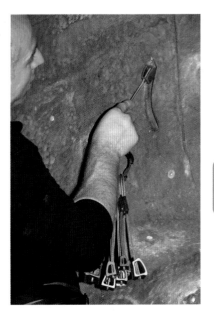

CLIPPING THE LOWER-OFF

Most routes will have what is called a 'finishing hold'. This will be a large jug that is easy to hold on to while making the clip into the lower-off point. Some walls also have a lip at the top, which allows you to hold on to the top of the wall itself. Whatever you do, make sure that you are well balanced (as for any clip) before taking a hand off to place the rope into the appropriate point.

(Above) **Placing protection when leading indoors**

(Below) **Most routes will have a large finishing jug next to the lower-off**

As far as the actual lower-off point is concerned there are many variations, but at the top of most leading routes will be at least a snapgate karabiner to allow for a rapid clip (very desirable at the top of a tricky lead!).

If you are just leading the route and then lowering off and pulling the rope down, either so that your companion can lead or because you are moving off to another climb, simply clipping the snapgate will suffice. Make sure that you are below the level of the karabiner, that the rope is fully clipped in and there is no way that the rope can run across the gate, thus unclipping itself. You can then be lowered to the ground from this one point.

Many lower-offs will consist of either two snapgates, with the openings facing in opposite directions, or a snapgate and a screwgate next to each other. You can clip in to both points when being lowered off, although this isn't always strictly necessary as pointed out above. However, this does become very important if the rope is going to be left in place so that you or

your companion can bottom-rope a route on the same line. Running a bottom-rope session with the rope just clipped in to a single snapgate is neither satisfactory nor safe (see Chapter 7 for photographs of various lower-offs).

Instructor's note

When teaching leading, a good way to progress from bottom-roping to true leading is by using a trail rope before your clients 'fly solo'. The only extra kit needed is a length of climbing rope, from 3m up to a full rope length. Have the climber tie on to the bottom rope as normal, then tie this second rope on as well. As they climb, safeguarded by the bottom rope, they can go through all the skills and techniques of clipping extenders on the lead but without the fear of falling. All the normal problems associated with leading – back-clipping, Z-clipping, stepping through and so on – can be ironed out in a safe environment. If working on a 1:1 basis the other advantage is that you can belay and your client will be able to experience leading the route without any of the usual concerns of managing not only a novice leader but also a belayer new to holding leader falls.

OVERHANGING ROUTES

Lowering off from the chains on overhanging routes has been mentioned above. However, you need to get there in the first place! Although very steep routes look intimidating, the big plus is that you are very unlikely to hit anything on the way down, so they represent a fairly safe way of pushing your grade. For instance, if you are trying to climb your first 6b and have a choice between a very delicate slab route and a more juggy one that overhangs, the latter may well be preferable as you might feel a bit safer on it in the case of a slip.

Clipping in to extenders can be tricky on overhangs, as you will have most of your weight hanging on one arm with very little respite being provided by your feet. Experiment a little with your body position, as to take even a small amount of weight off your arm by placing your feet on appropriate holds will make a big difference to how long you can stay on the wall. Hanging on a straight arm will usually be less tiring than hanging on a bent one as most of your body weight will be taken by your skeletal system and not your muscles, which would tire out relatively quickly.

If you need to rest during the climb, get near to your last clipped extender and pull yourself up and close to it before dropping off. If you are a distance away from it, when you let the rope take your weight you will very likely be unable to gain the wall again and have to be lowered down to the ground. You would then have to start the route again, possibly after untying and pulling the rope through, to gain your high point.

COMMUNICATION
Efficient communication is very important whether climbing indoors or out. A mix-up between belayer and climber can be the cause of an accident, so make sure that you and your climbing partner know what call is relevant in which situation.

Although the distances that you climb indoors will not normally be the same as those climbed outside on rock, there is still a need for clear calls. The echoing effect of the facility can make words hard to hear or distinguish; there may be music playing, noise from other climbers, other activities nearby (many walls share a hall with badminton courts, five-a-side football, volleyball and so on); for outdoor walls there may be traffic noise or wind. Having a clear call strategy with your climbing partner is important.

Be aware of who is around when walking below lead routes!

As the routes generally start and finish at the same point – on the ground – a complicated sequence of calls as may be used on outdoor rock climbs is not necessary. When you are next to your companion any conversation that clarifies what's happening will be fine – a simple 'ready' followed by an 'ok' will be fine; when you are separated by the height of the wall you need things to be a little more regimented. Even here, keep the calls to a minimum.

You may elect to use the sequence shown in the table below. Other variations exist but the important thing is that you agree the calls beforehand with your partner. Most are very similar to those used when bottom-roping, but they bear repeating here as they are important.

Leader	*I'm in.*	Called once the leader has clipped in to the lower-off
Belayer	*Ready?*	Called once the belayer has taken in all the slack, has most of the leader's weight and is ready to lower them.
Leader	*OK*	Confirmation that the leader is ready to descend.

A few calls may also be needed while the leader is climbing. Again, these can be any calls that are pre-agreed between the climber and belayer, but will probably be as follows:

Leader	*Slack!*	The belayer is holding the rope too tight, either when the climber is trying to move up or is pulling rope through to make a clip.
Leader	*Take in!*	There is excess rope in the system, maybe because the leader has down-climbed a little or was going to make a clip and has dropped the rope.
Leader	*Watch me!*	More reassurance for the leader (as the belayer should be watching them anyway); this shows that the leader is about to make a move, the outcome of which is not certain
Leader	*Take!*	Called as the leader falls off or rests on the rope.

Eye contact and a couple of simple hand signals may also be needed in noisy environments where calling to each other may not be an option.

TAKING FALLS

It is fairly inevitable at some stage in your leading career that you will fall off. Some would say that if you don't fall off frequently you are not trying hard enough to push your grade! That is probably true, but most of us have an inherent fear of falling and will do anything that we can to avoid it. However, the fear of falling will hold you back considerably when leading, and even climbing modest grade routes well within your ability can become daunting because of the fear factor.

So how do you go about overcoming this fear? Falling off a lot will help! Falling off will help you to build up a knowledge of what it feels like to drop off a route, how safe it is to do and how much trust you can have in your belayer. Fears arise from not knowing how much it will hurt when you stop, whether your knot will magically untie mid-flight, if the rope will snap or undo itself from the extenders and whether or not your belayer is holding on to the dead rope correctly. All of these possibly rational concerns can be negated by clocking up some 'flying time'.

- Choose an area of overhanging wall with big holds.

- Having tied on, make sure that your belayer is correctly positioned and will not be directly underneath you when you drop, and that the run of the rope is such that you will not end up catching a leg over it on the way down.

- Climb up and clip the first three extenders.

- While still below the third extender and without the rope being taken in tight, drop off. You will fall only a short distance before being gently stopped by the rope.

- Climb up again; this time pull a little slack through before dropping once more. You will travel a bit further but the deceleration will not be a problem. If you think about it, the more rope that is paid out the gentler the stop, as the rope absorbs a lot of the energy through elongation. Thus, the further you are away from the belayer the softer the stop will be.

- Climb a bit higher and clip the fourth extender.

- On and up a bit more, so that your waist is at the same level as the extender. Pull a bit more rope through and drop off. You will notice that this time you may ask your belayer three or four times if they are ready, as it does seem very high up! However, the effect of the drop and stop will be no more than it was earlier.

Once you have done this it is time to climb above the bolt, perhaps with it at knee or foot level, and fall off. This may be terrifying the first time, but continual practice will mean that you become more and more confident, and should soon be able to let go of the holds with little concern.

Once you have built up confidence on your 'tame' section of the wall, move along to another section of the overhang and repeat the process where you are above the extender when you fall off. This will help you to relax in the knowledge that you can fall safely from any part of the wall, whether you are familiar with it or not.

This falling practice and the confidence that it builds will pay huge dividends when on a route as you will feel far more comfortable in 'going for it' and pushing on a bit harder than you would have done before.

Note that holding a fall can also be worrying for the belayer. A couple of practice sessions are just as important for the belayer as it is for the leader, as they will also have a few 'unknowns' to deal with. How far will they fly up into the air? Will the belay device lock off or will there be a lot of rope slippage making the fall hard to hold? Once a few falls have been held and they discover that they do not fly into the air and that their belay device has worked properly (providing the correct belay device and rope combination has been used), the mystique will have gone out of it and they will be far more relaxed.

Instructor's note

When working with a novice team, one belaying and the other leading, pay particular attention to the belayer. As both will probably be nervous, being alongside the belayer will give the two of them a lot of confidence. In particular, loosely holding on to the dead end of the rope will make both of them feel happier and will help them to concentrate more on the climbing and belaying than any possible consequences.

Consider using a ground anchor for the belayer if that's appropriate, taking into consideration the direction of pull should a fall occur, and the load that will be exerted during the lower.

PARTNER CHECKS

As with bottom-roping, a system of partner checks is important. Make sure that the rope is tied in to the correct part of the harness and that the belay device is attached. If you are using a self-locking belay device, give it a test pull to make sure that the rope is oriented correctly – one less thing to worry about on your way up!

Instructor's checklist

When you are teaching lead climbing there are a lot of factors to take into consideration, and most of these should have been clarified in this chapter and Chapter 6.

You will have to work with a few novice leaders and belayers before you can come up with a full checklist of things that you need to look out for. There are obvious things that need to be done, such as making sure the partner check has been carried out, the consideration of ground anchors, holding the dead rope during the climb and giving advice to the leader. (For the latter move around as appropriate, as it will not be possible to see what is happening all the time from a position next to the belayer.)

There are a number of other important things to watch out for:

- The most common are the classic mistakes of Z-clipping, back-clipping and stepping through, although missing out clipping into extenders altogether happens quite frequently too. This latter problem is a mistake often made when moving from bottom-roping to leading, as the climber is so used to being involved in the

Confidently leading after all checks have been carried out

climbing and not having to worry about the rope that the fact that they have to clip it in on the move escapes them altogether! Keep a good eye on them; if they look as though they are moving past an extender, give them a shout.

- Make sure that the route that you choose for the climber's first lead is well within their comfortable bottom-roping grade, much easier than anything they would normally climb. Although competent climbers may scoff when pointed towards a grade 3 slab covered in large jugs, it is only by getting them to climb routes of a low grade that they will build up the skills of body positioning when clipping, balance and conservation of energy. Putting them on a hard route – even if they have been climbing hard on a bottom rope – will set them back a long way. Start it easy, and when both you and they are comfortable, move up the grades.

- Keep the belayer in mind and make sure that they are happy, as they will often be as stressed as a nervous leader. Make sure that the rope is placed in an appropriate position nearby and not strewn around the floor, and run it through beforehand to ensure it has no knot or kinks.

Remember that your clients will be watching what you do and will copy it. Thus, if you have a logical series of steps leading up to the climb – such as running the rope through, partner checks, belay device tug checks and the like – they will take these on board as part of their learning curve. This will get them into their own routine which in turn will help them to become safer and more efficient climbers which leads, at the end of the day, to having more fun!

See also Appendix 1 (Climber's checklist).

9 TOP-ROPING AND ABSEILING

This chapter is primarily intended for the use of instructors and wall staff, as it covers the technical skills needed for running top-rope and abseil sessions. These sessions will normally take place from dedicated abseil platforms built into the structure of the wall, but may also include abseil trees, buildings and the like.

They may be run for complete beginners or more experienced participants, in order to offer an extra dimension to their trip to the wall. However, usually only qualified instructors or wall staff members who have received extensive training can use abseil and top-rope platforms, due to the often complicated set-up and rigging skills needed, as well as the ability to run a safe session when working at height.

I will run through most of the methods that will be needed to run a successful session. However, it is how these methods are linked together that is important, and each climbing facility will be different. For instance, do your clients climb up and then walk off down the stairs at the back, or do they walk up them in order to abseil? Or perhaps they have to climb up to the ledge, there being no other way to access it, and then transfer to an abseil straight away to get back down? Although the skills of top-roping and abseiling remain essentially the same, it is how each individual facility lends itself to them that will ultimately decide how you rig and run the session.

EXTRA EQUIPMENT

Some extra items of equipment are useful for top-roping and abseiling sessions.

Maillons

Maillon

This is like a mini screwgate karabiner, and is useful when rigging anchor points and other sundry jobs. It is done up with a rotating sleeve, which can be securely tightened with a small spanner if necessary.

Figure of eight descender

This is a friction device designed to be used for abseiling. Its large surface area allows the heat generated by friction to dissipate easily, thus reducing any potential damage to the rope. For group abseils it may be a good idea to extend the figure of eight slightly so that it is held away from the abseiler, reducing the chance of hair, clothing and so on getting caught in it.

HMS screwgate karabiner

This becomes quite important here; the wide shape of this style of 'pear-shape' karabiner allows unimpeded use of an Italian hitch. If a standard D-shape karabiner was used the Italian hitch could jam during operation, causing all sorts of problems. It is worth having two or three of these to hand when rigging top-rope and abseil sessions. A photograph in Chapter 2 compares the two types.

WEAR A HELMET

Helmets will almost always be worn when abseiling, even if not used for climbing. The chance of someone flipping upside down has to be considered, and there is always the possibility of something being dropped from the ledge. The classic is something falling from an abseiler's pocket onto their friends watching below – being hit by a mobile telephone that has dropped 10m is not to be recommended!

Instructor's note

If you are going to be running a training session for other potential instructors, it is worth having a bit of spare kit with you. A bag that includes a few bolt hangers, an equal number of short bolts and an Allen key are very useful. These hangers can be attached to the wall in a quiet or cordoned-off area so that you can teach the basics of equalising anchors, rigging top-rope and abseil systems and so on while still on the ground in a controlled environment and with plenty of space. Once the basics have been demonstrated you can run the session from the abseil platform, often a place where space is quite limited.

Handled ascender

This is a useful piece of kit for ascending the rope when used in conjunction with a self-locking belay device. It is a specialist item which may be available for you to borrow from the climbing wall. They come in left- and right-handed

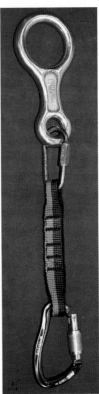

Figure of eight descender, extended with a maillon and short sling

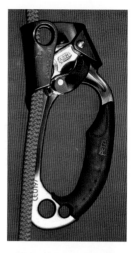

(Left) **Handled ascender**
(Right) **Dedicated abseil ledge;
note the sliding gate and ropes
pre-rigged to strong-points**

versions, so if you are going to buy one choose the one that best suits your purpose.

EXTRA TECHNICAL SKILLS

Some further technical skills that need to be covered, on top of those detailed previously.

Equalising anchors

Although some abseil ledges that are used frequently will have kit permanently rigged, many will consist of just a couple of bolt hangers from which you need to set up your climbing and abseiling systems. It is normal practice to link two bolts together for reasons of safety, with each bolt taking 50 percent of the load.

Chain and maillon rig

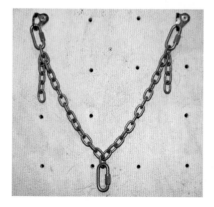

One method is to use a dedicated **chain and maillon rig**. This will be worth purchasing if you are running a lot of sessions at either one or a number of different venues. Its advantages are that it is almost indestructible (important in a piece of kit designed to be used frequently), it can be adjusted to a variety of lengths, and it offers a number of places into which temporary attachment can be made for personal safety when rigging, swapping clients over and so on.

Make sure that both the chain and maillons used are strength rated in excess of the loadings that they will have to hold.

Another system uses a couple of **screwgate karabiners and a sling**, the length of which will commonly be 120cm (often called an '8-foot' sling), or 240cm (often called a '16-foot' sling). The centimetre measurement refers to the sling when flat, the feet measurement refers to the circumference. Slings tend to be sold using the former specification.

Place a screwgate karabiner into each of the bolts and use one of the following methods. The first method is quick, simple and versatile.

(Left) **Equalising anchors using the overhand knot method**
(Centre) **Overhand knot with one loop longer than the other, useful when rigging an abseil.**
(Right) **Equalising anchors using the single overhand knot method**

- Clip the sling in to the bolts.
- Decide where you want the attachment point for the rig to be and, holding both sections of sling together, tie an overhand knot (or a figure of eight – easier to untie afterwards), on the bight of sling.
- This will be your central attachment point for any karabiners supporting the rest of the rig.

If you are using this method to rig for an abseil, it would be advantageous to have the two loops of the knot of unequal length, with one approximately 30cm longer than the other. The reason for rigging it like this will become apparent during the abseiling section below.

A second method of using a sling comes in handy if the anchors are a bit further apart.

- Clip one end of the sling in to one anchor and estimate where you will need the central attachment point.
- At that point, tie a simple overhand knot around the sling.
- Clip it to the second anchor to create two mini-slings.
- Clip a screwgate karabiner either side of the overhand knot, taking care that you are going through the sling and not just around it.

Note

A long sling, such as 240cm, is very useful when rigging. You can shorten it to any length you may need very simply by tying an overhand knot in it and clipping the resulting loop in to the anchors.

LOCKING OFF THE ITALIAN HITCH

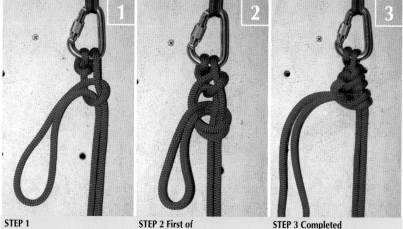

STEP 1
Slippery hitch

STEP 2 First of
two half hitches

STEP 3 Completed
locked-off Italian hitch

- If you need to, adjust the overhand knot one way or another until the load point is where you want it.

Although this is a quick and useful method, the main disadvantage is that you cannot form two uneven loops as mentioned above.

Locking off the Italian hitch

This is needed when running abseil sessions as it will be used to secure the abseil rope to the anchor. It can also be used in an emergency situation; an advantage is that this can be done when the hitch is loaded with a climber's body weight, although it will take a little practice to be able to tie it and release it without causing any slippage.

As you tie each section, pull it up snug against the karabiner. Also make sure that when you have finished there is at least 30cm of loop left over, as this ensures that the knot will be secure.

GAINING THE ABSEIL LEDGE

By far the easiest way to do this will be to nip up the stairs that have been provided precisely for this purpose! However, failing that – and without the luxury of an internal ladder and trapdoor – you will have to approach the ledge from below, either by climbing the wall or by ascending the rope. The pros and cons of the various ways in which this can be done are outlined below.

METHOD	PROS	CONS
Soloing	Fast, needs no equipment, needs no other person.	Danger of injury or death if a fall is taken, reliant upon route grade being climbable, danger of holds spinning, poor demonstration to novice group, carrying of kit needs to be thought through.
Belayed on climb	Potentially safe.	Needs competent belayer, grade of route to be appropriate, relies on rope being in place for bottom-roped ascent, needs competence in leading if no rope in place.
Ascending the rope	Potentially safe, needs no other person, grade of route immaterial.	Takes practice to set up and become slick, possibility of slippage if diameter of rope not compatible with ascension device, relies on rope being in place.

Soloing is by far the most dangerous, and although it is potentially the fastest way up to the ledge it could prove to be the fastest way down as well! Being belayed by a competent person is certainly a good way to gain a ledge, as long as they know what you will be doing once you arrive at the top, and can manage the rope effectively. This competent person may be one of the wall staff if available.

As most sessions will be run with one instructor to the group, and as wall staff often have other things to do, ascending the rope will often be the best way up. This is the same method used by route setters to gain the top of the wall prior to rigging their working rope systems.

It is common to use a self-locking belay device to climb the rope. Although there are a number of mechanical ascenders available on the market, these are designed to be pushed up the rope. A belay device is designed to have the rope pulled through it, which is what will happen here. Make sure that the device you choose is appropriate for the thickness of rope in place.

Assuming a top-rope is already in place on your wall, here is a common method of ascending it:

- Tie on to the climbing rope.
- Clip an appropriate device on to the side of the rope coming down from the top anchor.
- Clip the device into your abseil or tie-in loop with a screwgate karabiner. Make sure that any moving parts of the device cannot be inhibited by your body, other parts of your harness and so on. If this is a possibility, extend the device away from you a little using an extender with a screwgate karabiner at each end.
- Pulling on the dead rope and using the wall for your feet if at all possible, move on up. You can sit back in your harness so that you can change your hand position whenever necessary.

TOP-ROPING AND ABSEILING

- Remember to tie in short.
- Tie an overhand knot every subsequent couple of metres as you ascend.

Although this method is very common, you can refine it slightly and make the ascent of very steep or overhanging routes a lot easier. An extra piece of kit in the form of a handled ascender is needed here.

- Have the rope and self-locking belay device set up as described above.
- Place a handled ascender on the rope running to your harness, above the belay device.
- Clip a screwgate karabiner into the lowest point of the handled ascender.
- The dead rope coming from the belay device is run up through the screwgate and allowed to hang down.
- To move up, pull down on the handled device and pull on the dead rope coming from the screwgate. This will lift you up, particularly if you can get foot contact with the wall.
- Relax onto the belay device so that it takes your weight – it should lock off automatically.
- Push the handled ascender further up the rope and then repeat the process.

It is very important that you back up your ascent in case the system slips. There are two simple ways to do this:

- Remember to tie in short.
- Have a sling lark's footed on to the handled ascender, the other end of which is clipped in to your abseil loop. If your self-locking belay device should slip, this will stop you from going any distance.

On the steepest ground you may also wish to hang a sling or short length of rope with a loop in the end from the handled ascender as a foot loop (this must be the correct length for you to use, so make it adjustable until you have the length right). Place one foot in it and stand up as you pull down on the handled ascender and pull on the dead rope. This will make even free-hanging ascents quite easy.

Personal safety on the ledge

This is a crucial aspect that should not be overlooked or taken for granted. The instructor will move about on the ledge a lot while rigging and during top-roping or abseiling, so it is essential to be clipped in.

If there is no safeguarding system already set up on the ledge, such as a pre-rigged rope with an attachment point at an appropriate place, the simplest and most common method will be to use a cow's tail.

Another useful type of sling is called a '**daisy chain**'. This has a series of loops sewn along its length and is handy when you need to adjust the distance between the anchor and you every now and then. It is essential that you clip through just one loop section and not through two adjacent ones; if you did the latter your weight would be taken just by the stitching creating the loops and not by the sling itself. This could fail if it were subject to loading, such as would be created if you slipped from the ledge.

Note

It is essential that the camming action of a Grigri is not inhibited by the knot that is tied on your harness. These devices are commonly used at climbing walls, so you need to know how to use them to ascend safely. As the cam is on the left-hand side of the Grigri, make sure that it is on the left-hand side of the knot when you attach it, so that it can move freely. If there is any question, choose another device that doesn't have a moving cam on the exterior, such as an Eddy.

Using a daisy chain as a cow's tail

....

If using a 120cm sling as your cow's tail it is worth tying an overhand knot in it approximately 30cm from your harness. This will be useful when abseiling from the ledge at the end of the session, so it's handy to have it tied ready in place.

BRINGING UP EQUIPMENT

If you need to fully equip the ledge with ropes, karabiners, slings and assorted paraphernalia needed to run a top-roping or abseil session, you obviously need to get it up there somehow! Although it would be possible to attach a lot of it to your harness and carry the ropes on your back, make life easy for yourself and bring it up after you have arrived. One possibility will be to tie the whole lot to the dead end of the rope that you are going to climb up to gain the ledge in the first place. Once you are up and secured, pull the rope up and the kit will follow. A problem here is that kit, and in particular ropes, will tend to catch on protruding holds, making the process laborious if not impossible. To solve this, uncoil the ropes on the floor before you leave and just tie one end to the rope you are ascending; there will be far less chance of anything snagging. Another option is to use a haul bag or rucksack. Put all the kit inside, tie it to the end of the rope and pull it up once you are safely ensconced.

TOP-ROPING

Once you are set up and safe on the ledge, you can prepare the top-rope system. This is often best done with an Italian hitch on the anchor, as this provides a quick, safe and secure way of looking after the climber.

- Run the climbing rope through to make sure that there are no knots or kinks. As you do so, pile it out of the way so that it can't be trodden on or tripped over.
- Lower sufficient rope down to reach the ground.
- Clip a large HMS screwgate into the central point of the anchor.
- Clip an Italian hitch into the HMS and you are ready to go.

Belaying with an Italian hitch

This knot is frequently used for top-roping as it is easy to operate. Remember that the maximum friction within the knot is created by holding the ropes parallel which, as you should always rig it with the Italian hitch behind you and away from the edge, will be easy to do. It is important that the dead rope is never let go, so practise belaying up the rope with no one on it until you get the technique sorted.

Two methods will work; the first seems to be the most popular.

BELAYING WITH AN ITALIAN HITCH – METHOD 1

  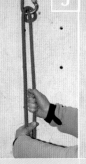 

| STEP 1 Starting position | STEP 2 Feeding the rope into the Italian hitch | STEP 3 The left hand has slid down the live rope to grip the dead rope between thumb and forefinger | STEP 4 The hand on the dead rope is slid up to near the Italian hitch | STEP 5 The dead rope is released by the left hand; then back to the starting position |

- Start with your dead hand near the hitch and your live hand further down the rope.
- Pull the rope up with your live hand and pull the slack through the hitch with your dead hand.
- Once your live hand is close to the hitch, slide it back down the rope so that it is a little beyond your dead hand.
- Using just thumb and forefinger on your live hand, grip the rope below your dead hand.
- Slightly release the grip of your dead hand (do not let go), and slide it back up to the hitch.
- Release the rope between thumb and forefinger of your live hand, and you are ready to repeat the process.

The following alternative is useful if the anchor is high (see photographs on the next page).

- Start as before and pull the rope through the hitch.
- When your live hand is close to the hitch, take it off and place it between the hitch and your dead hand.
- Take your dead hand off the rope and replace it between your other hand and the hitch.
- Now move your original live hand back to its starting position on the live rope.

Note

Make sure that neither hand gets too close to the Italian hitch. It will roll over when loaded, and if you have a hand close your skin could get trapped between the hitch and the karabiner, held there by some-one's body weight. Not to be recommended!

BELAYING WITH AN ITALIAN HITCH – METHOD 2

STEP 1 Starting to take the rope in	STEP 2 Feeding the rope into the Italian hitch	STEP 3 Both hands on the dead rope	STEP 4 Swapping hands	STEP 5 Back to the starting position

Both hands on the dead rope, ready to pay out

Note

This method of attachment, where a karabiner or two are used to attach the rope to the harness, must only ever be used where the system will never be shock-loaded, such as in top- and bottom-roping. It must never be used as an attachment method for lead climbing.

It will also be necessary to pay out using the Italian hitch. To do this, place both hands on the dead rope and shuffle the rope through slowly and steadily, just as you would with a belay device.

Connecting the group to the rope

Once on the ledge there is the question of how to attach your group members to the rope each time a different person wants to climb. Tying on is always going to be the best bet, but you must be absolutely certain that they all know how to tie on safely. This will be easy with one or two people with whom you have been working closely, but working with a group of novices brings different challenges. Tying on in this case will be fine if you have a helper on the ground who knows what they are doing, but this will rarely be the case.

Clipping clients in to their abseil loop with a screwgate karabiner is the answer, but once again be careful how you do this. Some harness manufacturers state that two karabiners, not just one, should be used when connecting the rope to the harness in this way (see Chapter 7) to prevent one karabiner being subjected to a sideways loading should it slip round during the climb. Another answer to the sideways loading problem is to use a karabiner that is designed in such a way that it cannot rotate sideways (such as a Belay Master).

A standard check is called a 'squeeze test'. Once the climber has the karabiner/s connected to their harness take in any slack rope so that it is snug to them. Get them

to hold the karabiner across the gate and back bar and squeeze. If they have not done the screwgate up correctly the gate will open, so make sure that you are watching carefully and get them to screw the gate up if this occurs, and do the test again.

Climbing calls

The group should be briefed as to what climbing calls you are going to use. Make sure that they understand that they must not climb until you are ready and the agreed sequence of calls have been carried out. Keep the calls simple otherwise people will forget them; they can be reduced to just a couple as you will have line of sight of the climber, can see that they are connected to the rope and that the slack has been taken in.

Climb when you are ready.	A call from the belayer once the rope has been taken in, the squeeze test carried out and checks on the ledge finished.
Climbing!	Called by the climber, but they do not start climbing until they have heard...
OK!	Called by the belayer to show that everything is ready and they are paying full attention to the climber.

Lowering a climber

Once you have your climber with you – and assuming there is no stair access – they obviously needs to go back down. Chances are that you have also rigged an abseil and they will transfer onto that, but if not you will need to lower them.

This is easy to do with the Italian hitch.

Lowering with a Grigri. Note the rope being fed into the device from behind with a karabiner clipped in to the anchor: B = belayer, C = climber. It is essential that the cam can move freely

- Get them in a comfortable position, facing you with their feet on top of the wall or some other suitable ledge.
- Have both your hands on the dead rope and shuffle them up and down so that the rope is paid out smoothly. A one-inch slip feels like a six-foot drop to the person on the end of the rope, so take it steady!
- Get them to sit back in his harness, feet at least shoulder width and legs straight, walking down as you pay the rope out. They can hold on to the knot on their harness if they feel they have to, but make sure that they don't grab any hold on the wall on the way down, as they could end up staying there!

Another option is to use a self-locking device in place of the Italian hitch. The advantage of this is that it will not tend to twist the rope when the person is climbing towards you. The downside is that it takes a bit of management to get climbers lowering off, if that is how they are descending, smoothly. It is also not a good way to protect a person if they are going to transfer to the abseil rig and go down on that. Make sure that you are using the device in a manner where the moving parts are able to move freely, and that you understand how to set the device up for lowering.

DESCENDING FROM THE LEDGE

This is one of the most dangerous times for instructors, who are descending from height after (perhaps) a long session on the ledge and have other things on their mind (such as group management and the impending end of the session). It is here that mistakes can be made; take great care, think things through carefully and double-check everything.

There are a variety of methods of descending, and the trick is to do it under control!

Option 1 Reverse what you did to get there in the first place. If you had someone belay you up and you planned ahead, you will have the end of the rope secured near the ledge so can get your belayer ready, tie back in, unclip your cow's tail and down-climb. This will likely be the quickest and safest method of getting down.

Option 2 If there is no one else around – or no one competent enough to belay – you will have to come up with another plan. Abseiling will usually be the answer, and here we will look at two forms: a reversal of getting up there (when you used an Eddy or similar device), or an abseil in the true sense.

If you used the **rope and an ascender** to get to the ledge, you will presumably still have the device with you.

- Retie on to the end of the rope (which you will have attached to part of the anchor or other suitable point on the ledge).
- Clip the Eddy (or whatever you used to get there) on to the rope running down on the opposite side of the top anchor.
- Give everything a test tug to make sure that all is well and oriented correctly.
- If the back-up knots that you tied in the rope as you made your way up are still there all well and good. If they have been taken out – perhaps because people have been using the rope to climb on while you have been busy – pull the rope up and tie a couple of knots as backups a few metres apart some way down. This is important if the rope's diameter is at the lower limit for your device.
- After a final check that everything is locking off as it should, unclip your cow's tail, clip it out of the way on the side of your harness, and descend.
- Before getting to each of the knots, stop, pull the rope up a little and remove them.

It may be that you have to make a **'proper' abseil** to get down from the ledge. This could be on the bottom rope that you used to get up there, or may be a rope that you have been using, doubled and run around a suitable part of the anchor system. Generally, the rope that you abseil on will be doubled so you can then pull it down after you, or use it for re-ascent depending upon the situation. However, some ledges will have a single rope permanently in place for descending.

You could use either a figure of eight descender or a belay device to abseil with. For the sake of this description, let's assume that a belay device is being used and the rope that you are going to abseil on is doubled and run around a strong point of the ledge system, to be retrieved later.

- While still attached to the anchor with your cow's tail, put the abseil device on both ropes.
- Clip it to your cow's tail. This is where the overhand knot tied in the sling approximately 30cm from your harness (mentioned above), comes in useful, as you will clip the device into the small loop thus formed. Do up the screwgate (an HMS is desirable here).
- Now place a French Prusik on the dead rope coming out from, and hanging below, your abseil device. Four or five wraps should do the trick; practise this beforehand. Clip this to the abseil loop on your harness. You now have a 'dead man's handle' so that you don't lose control on the way down.

- Having checked the system screwgates and so on and had a test tug, unclip your cow's tail, store it on the side of your harness and descend.
- The best way to abseil is to have one hand holding the loops of the Prusik slack, the other controlling your descent with the dead rope. Avoid the temptation to use just one hand on the way down, as this will give a very jerky journey. Having the rope between your legs and not off to one side will also help smooth things out.

It is obviously possible to abseil without placing the Prusik around the ropes as an emergency brake, and you may well elect to do this for most of your descents. However, if you are going to be abseiling for any distance or the descent is tricky – perhaps it is from an abseil tree and there are branches to negotiate, or the section of indoor wall that you have to go down is overhanging or simply a long way down – then backing up your abseil device is a very good precaution.

Abseil rig using a Prusik back-up; note the extended section of the cow's tail clipped to the side of the harness

Top-rope rig with an Italian hitch; the belayer has her cow's tail attached to a separate anchor

GROUP ABSEILING

If there is not a dedicated abseil rig already in place, this can be set up on the same anchor system as the top rope. Apart from your own safety cow's tail (discussed above) there will be two main elements, the abseil rope and the safety rope. It may be that the safety rope that you are going to use for the abseil has already been used as the top rope for a climb, with the person simply clipping on to a descender and heading back on down.

Instructor's note

You may be up on the ledge for some time when running a session. Walls are notoriously dusty; you will be taking almost constantly, encouraging and directing your group, and you will certainly get thirsty quickly. Taking a drink up with you is a good idea, along with a bite to eat if you are going to be there for a prolonged period.

Rigging the abseil rope

Abseil ropes will generally (though not always), be of the low-stretch variety. This means that they are not as elastic as standard climbing ropes and as such are quite hard wearing as well as being cheaper than the dynamic ropes generally used for climbing.

- Clip an HMS karabiner into the central point of the anchor.
- Unflake the abseil rope and run it through to check that there are no knots or kinks.
- Lower one end of the rope off the ledge until it is about 0.5m off the ground.
- Tie an Italian hitch in it and clip this to the HMS karabiner. (The reason for attaching the abseil rope with a tied-off Italian hitch is so that it can be released if a problem is encountered (see p158).)
- Check that the Italian hitch is oriented to be on the abseil-rope side of the karabiner (as opposed to being on the spare-rope side), and lock it off as detailed in 'Top-roping', above.
- Place the spare rope away from people's feet in a loose pile, and that's the system set up.

Rigging the safety rope

This will also go on to the central point of the anchor system. It is very handy if it can be clipped in to a slightly extended part of the system, so that when both the abseil rope and the safety rope are loaded the Italian hitches do not rub together. It is for this reason that it was earlier suggested that the overhand knot of a sling is tied in unequal lengths, with the abseil rope on the shorter one and the safety rope on the longer one.

- Clip an HMS in to a suitable part of the anchor.
- Run the safety rope through to check that there are no knots or kinks in it.
- Tie a figure of eight knot and stopper knot in the end of the safety rope.
- Add a screwgate karabiner to the end of the rope
- Connect the safety rope to the HMS with an Italian hitch, check that the gate is done up, and that's it finished.

Running the session

We will assume for the moment that the abseiler is with you on the ledge, having got there by means other than climbing up.

Note
. . . .

Although the abseil rope and safety rope are usually run from the same equalised anchor, there is no reason why, if you can rig two separate anchor systems side by side or one above the other, that you don't do this instead. You may find it easier to keep the two sections of the system apart and have more space to work in.

Overview of the abseil and safety ropes rigged for a session; two separate anchors have been used

- Make sure that the abseiler is in a designated safe area and clipped to any safety system that is provided.
- Place the descender high up on the abseil rope so that the person will not be hanging over the edge once they are connected.
- With the Italian hitch in place and a hand holding the dead rope (keep this on here all the time now), reach across and clip the safety rope karabiner into their abseil loop.
- Have a final check of their harness and helmet.
- Having released them from the safe-area safety system, bring them forward, taking the safety rope in as necessary, and clip the descender to their abseil loop above the safety rope karabiner.
- Have a final check of the system and off they go.

That's all well and good if they have pottered up a staircase to get to you, but what if they climbed up on a top rope (which will often be the case)? Remember that they will probably have brought up the figure of eight that the last person used to abseil with, so you need to connect it to the abseil rope once they have arrived.

Note
. . . .
It will take a bit of forward planning to not get in a tangle with the ropes, especially on small ledges. Think ahead, decide from which side the abseiler will be approaching, how the safety rope will be running, and so on. Always take time to get everything running smoothly, even if you have to get the group to step back from the edge while you rearrange a part of the system. You should soon be able to make a judgement based on experience as to how to rig the system so as to avoid any problems.

- Have a short cow's tail pre-rigged to the anchor, with a screwgate karabiner on it. This should be of an appropriate length so that the climber/abseiler cannot slip off the ledge.
- Flick the abseil rope off to one side of their route up so that it doesn't get in the way as they climb.
- Bring them up.
- When they arrive at the ledge, clip them in to the cow's tail.
- You can now have hands free to retrieve the figure of eight from them and connect it to the abseil rope.
- Flick the abseil rope back into line.
- Clip the figure of eight onto their abseil loop.
- After a final check, hold the dead side of the safety rope, release them from the cow's tail and down they go!

Stacking the group on the ledge
An alternative to having the group climb up and then abseil straight back down would be to get them on the ledge while everyone climbs and they then abseil one after the other. It is quite exciting to be sitting high up and can add an extra dimension to your session. The deciding factors will most likely be the size of the ledge and the availability of anchors for the group to clip in to.

The safety of the group is paramount. You could equip each person with their own cow's tail; although this will work for a couple of folk, more than that and it gets a bit awkward. There is also the concern of group members tripping over the sling as they climb. A better option will be to set up a rope system in to which they can clip with a karabiner. You can use either a short length of rope or a section of a climbing rope.

- Tie a figure of eight into one end and clip it into a suitable part of the anchor.
- Tie a series of overhand knots with long loops on the rope, one for each person. Make sure that there is enough length of loop for them to be comfortable but not so much that they can fall any distance.
- Secure the far end of the rope to the anchor, preferably a different section.

- Either equip each person with a screwgate or, better still, clip one on to each of the loops.
- When each person arrives, keep him or her on the safety rope until clipped in and the squeeze test done.
- You can now take the rope off them and get the next person up.

Make sure that you 'stack' the group in the order that you want them to take off again down the abseil. This will normally mean the first person being nearest to you, as long as there is space. Having arrived first they will then leave first. However, this system is quite flexible and as everyone is very close the order can easily be changed.

Note

You will most likely need to retrieve the descender each time the abseiler has had a go. Instead of getting them to clip it to the safety rope and dragging it up the wall, provide a small canvas bag with a loop on that they can use. This clips onto the back of their harness as they go down and, once they have taken the abseil device off the rope, they clip the bag onto the safety rope, put the abseil device into it and you can pull it up again. This not only reduces the chance of kit becoming stuck on protruding holds, it also keeps wall staff happier as you are not clunking their expensive climbing wall with a lump of swinging metal!

Tip

The abseil rope has been rigged so that it is a little way off the ground. This is so that, when the person reaches the ground, you can pull up on the abseil rope thus unwrapping it from the descender. They then just have to unscrew the karabiner instead of trying to get the rope from around the device, which some people find tricky.

Avoiding problems

As long as you have rigged the system properly, briefed the group appropriately and planned ahead, there should be very little that can go wrong. Perhaps the commonest problem is someone refusing to commit to the abseil and not wanting to go down. If they climbed up there in the first place on a top rope this is very unlikely, but if they arrived via a staircase then this may be their (very understandable!) reaction. After time spent trying to coax them over the edge (in relation to the overall time available for the group session – trying for 40 minutes to get someone to abseil when there are five others waiting and it is only an hour-long session won't go down very well), get them well away from the edge before unclipping them from the system. You may find that, after watching a couple of their friends abseil, the nervous person wants to have another try, which is absolutely great. Give them the opportunity, as having seen others do it may give them the impetus to have a go.

Most other problems should have been solved before they happen, and that is where the real skill is involved. As far as technique is concerned, if the group has been climbing elsewhere, they should be happy with the abseil position as they will probably have been lowered off a few climbs already. However, if not, you may be able to save yourself – and them – a lot of time and stress by rigging up a quick demonstration at ground level. Show them how to operate the figure of eight, the correct position to adopt, the role of the safety rope and, very importantly, what to do with all of the kit – unclipping and so on – when they reach the ground. This may seem time-consuming but it will save a lot of time in the long run, and will help the session to run more smoothly and give people the chance of plenty of goes during the session.

Releasing the abseil rope in an emergency

This is a procedure that you may have to carry out and that you need to have practised beforehand. It is the classic problem, beloved of instructor training and assessment courses, but should be avoidable with efficient planning and observation. It will probably happen because someone has caught their hair in the abseil device and their weight is hanging from it, an extremely painful occurrence that needs to be sorted out very quickly. However, the skill lies in preventing it in the first place, and observation of your group – in particular when doing a helmet check – should give you a warning. It is worth having a few spare hair ties available for anyone with particularly long hair.

However, it is sensible to go through the process of solving the problem should it, despite your best efforts, occur.

An abseiler has descended a distance when suddenly some of their hair gets pulled in through the figure of eight. The noise they make is impressive!

- Immediately hold the safety rope with both hands, being careful to not let go of the dead rope, and pull upwards, using your legs for power. Nine times out of 10 this will solve the problem, as it takes their weight off the abseil rope momentarily so they can pull their hair through.
- If this does not solve the problem, maybe because they are very heavy, you are slight or the abseil is overhanging, take the safety rope in tight.
- Hold the dead rope parallel with the live rope, thus providing maximum friction and security.
- With your free hand undo the locked-off Italian hitch. Take care with the slippery hitch as it will pull through a little with their body weight, so keep your fingers clear.

- Once you have released the locked-off section, pull some abseil rope through so that there is slack going down to the abseiler. They will then be able to release their hair.
- Lower them to the ground on the safety rope. Note that the abseil rope will probably run through the Italian hitch as you lower them; let it do so. It is better to get them to the ground before you re-rig the system rather than trying to do it while they are hanging there.

A TECHNICAL RESCUE

If things go terribly wrong in either a top-roping or abseiling situation you may have to resort to what's known as a 'crag snatch' or a 'Y-hang rescue'. This really is right at the end of the line and is highly technical thing, indicative that you have tried everything else but nothing has worked.

Say that someone has, for some reason, become completely stuck part way up or down the wall, taken their weight off the rope and is refusing to move. This will be more common on a climb than an abseil because with the latter they have already committed themselves to the system, so is likely to be happy to continue to do so. On a climb, the rope to them may be stretchy, causing them to lose confidence.

The good news is that you will probably have enough rope on the ledge with you. If it is a top-rope situation, you can go down on the pile of rope on the dead-end side of the belay system. If it is an abseil, you have three choices:

- The back end of the safety rope.
- The back end of the abseil rope.
- You could also pull through a little of the live rope that the abseiler is on (as the stuck climber is on a ledge, the system is not weighted), and go down on that.

In either a climbing or abseiling scenario there may also be a spare rope on the ledge that you can use, although this is unlikely.

We will look at this scenario from a climbing perspective (dealing with an abseiler is very similar).

- You have decided that you have no option but to go down. Pull in any slack (which you should have done already to help encourage them), and lock off the Italian hitch.
- On the dead rope from the Italian hitch, tie a figure of eight on the bight and clip this on to a suitable part of the anchor. It is the rope coming out of this that you will go down on.

Note

Being able to make a crag snatch quickly and efficiently is great, as we all enjoy playing with ropes, knots and the like. However, it is a last resort after all else has failed; coaxing, talking, encouraging and possibly utilising bribery (chocolate!), should all have been tried before you start out.

STEP 1 Clipping through the cow's tail sling in the correct manner

STEP 2 Figure of eight clipped from the back of the locked-off Italian hitch

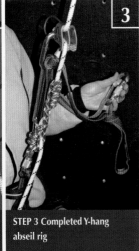

STEP 3 Completed Y-hang abseil rig

- Prepare yourself for the abseil. Attach your device to the rope you are going to abseil on and clip it in to your cow's tail sling. It is very important that the karabiner is clipped through both sides of the sling, both in to the small loop to your harness (as for a personal abseil) and also in to the larger loop on to which you will clip the victim (and which is most likely currently clipped into the anchor as your personal safety).
- Put a French Prusik on the dead rope under your abseil device.
- Deploy the rope down the wall. This will be best done by lowering it rather than throwing it off. Make sure that there is no one underneath and that the rope touches the ground.
- Have a final check that the victim is definitely not going to move (they may have changed their mind).
- Assuming they haven't, have a final check of the system.
- Unclip your personal safety and tie another knot in the sling to shorten it to about the same length as the one to your harness.
- Clip your personal safety karabiner on to the shortened section of sling and then on to a suitable point, such as a gear loop or into the karabiner holding your abseil device. This will be needed shortly for the victim to clip in to.
- Carefully abseil to the victim, stopping a bit above them.
- With the spare end of the sling now unclipped from your harness, inch your way down until you can reach down and clip it in to their abseil loop.

- Now take a few wraps of the rope around your thigh so that you can comfortably take your hands off while you work.
- Untie them from the climbing rope.
- Coax them back so that they are hanging from the spare end of your sling. This will often have to be done with an arm at the back of their harness.
- Once their weight is on your rope, abseil to the ground.

Instructor's note

At the end of the session, make sure that your group knows what is happening, and that you have briefed them as to what to do. It may take you some time to de-rig the equipment, lower it down and then abseil. Do you know where your group is? Is it a group of young people wandering around a busy climbing centre, in danger of being fallen on? Have they taken themselves off bouldering and are high above the floor? Brief them at a suitable stage as to what to do while you are de-rigging. If you are not travelling home with them it may be worth descending straight away, finishing the session and then going back up to collect the kit.

Instructor's note

When you are on a ledge – particularly one that is small – it is very easy for loose kit to be knocked off by feet or to be flicked off by the rope. Make sure that everything is secured, most usefully done by clipping it in to some part of the system. If there are likely to be loose items around – perhaps the group has asked you to take a couple of cameras up with you – it would be useful to have a small bag with a sewn loop that can be clipped back into the anchor. An old stuff sack with a strong cord would be handy here.

Tip

When using a sling to equalise anchors, use one that is thick and broad, rather than a thin and light Dyneema variety. Although these have their place in climbing, when they have been loaded, particularly during an abseil session, any knots that you have tied in them are an absolute nightmare to untie again.

Note

When equalising an anchor, make sure that the angle at the knot described by the two sides of the sling as they go to the bolts is 90 degrees or less. Much more than this and you will be greatly increasing the load on each side of the system and lose the advantage of having two anchors in the first place.

Competing at an outdoor dry tooling competition on a man-made tower.
Note that crampons are being worn, rarely done indoors

10 DRY TOOLING

Centres offering dry tooling – which is becoming a very popular sport – have found an efficient way of maximising the use of wall space. Dry tooling is the use of ice axes to cross ground that has no snow or ice on it. In a practical sense, this means climbing indoors on standard bolt-on or wooden holds, either on existing bottom-rope lines or in dedicated dry tooling areas.

This type of climbing is very powerful and gives rise to a number of spectacular and strenuous techniques, which will be examined later in this chapter.

Although dry tooling would not be possible without the use of an axe in each hand, it will usually be carried out without crampons, wearing standard rock shoes (or often mountain boots when competing). This is generally for reasons of safety, as to catch a crampon point on the wall during a fall, or to land on one when tooling across the roof of a bouldering cave, would almost certainly result in injury. Some walls may have areas where crampons are used, although these are often exclusively on walls made from natural rock, and where bottom-roping is the norm.

Dry tooling is very useful for practising winter climbing techniques, but many climbers now view it as a skill in its own right. Dry tooling caves and walls have their own dedicated band of aficionados who spend hours working out a sequence of moves, just as boulderers do with problems in conventional bouldering areas.

Most climbing facilities with a dry tooling area will require climbers to undergo a formal induction session. This will cover topics such as the correct use of the equipment, dos and don'ts specific to the climbing wall, as well as basic safety information.

EQUIPMENT

Axes
Most climbers will start out with a standard set of climbing axes, often consisting of one hammer and one adze, exactly the same as for winter climbing. However, a new generation of axes, designed specifically for the purpose of dry tooling, has evolved, and will make a huge difference as to how hard

Dedicated dry tooling axes;
note the absence of either
hammer or adze

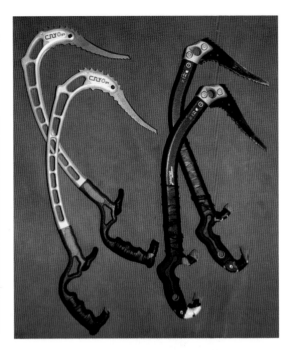

Tip

If you are going to use your own ice axes it is worth protecting yourself from injury by taking off the hammer and adze sections. If this is not possible think about covering them with some foam and tape so that, should an axe ping off a hold and hit you in the face, you won't get injured.

or easy specific moves will feel. If you have no axes of your own these can often be hired for a small charge (along with other essential items of equipment) from the climbing wall.

As one of the major benefits of dry tooling is the ease with which axes can be swapped from hand to hand, leashes are not used in the majority of cases. For this reason dedicated axes have a very pronounced bend to the shaft, often more like a right angle, which gives a comfortable grip. This also allows the maximum leverage to be applied to the tip of the axe pick, essential when trying to stay in contact with the smallest of holds.

Most axes will also have a 'trigger' grip, which allows you to hold on to a variety of points up the shaft, essential when performing some of the more technical moves such as changing hands and short-tooling.

Helmet

This is important; being hit on the head by a flailing axe, or having one dropped on your head by your climbing partner when bottom-roping, would certainly ruin your day! An everyday climbing helmet, or one that has been designed for dry tooling and has built-in protection, are both suitable. This protection may consist of either a metal grid covering the face or a Perspex visor protecting the eyes. Bear in mind that even if wearing one with a metal grid a very unlucky

climber could still find an axe pick poking them in the eye (see Eye protection below).

Helmet with full visor to give protection from flying axes

Eye protection

This is essential. If protection is not built in to your helmet, a pair of industrial quality safety glasses will be ideal, and these can be purchased from your local builder's merchants. Pay for good quality and look after them, as scratched glasses are very annoying to use.

Clear plastic goggles could also be used, although these tend to make your face a bit sweaty and aren't as comfortable for a prolonged period of time.

Gloves

Gloves are important to help your grip on the axe and to negate the chance of skinning a knuckle. However, these need to be thin so that your hands do not slide around in them, as well as giving more control over the axe. Although dedicated dry tooling gloves are available, the best option is a pair of tight-fitting mountain-bike gloves, available from your local cycling shop. These tend to do up tightly and minimise hand slippage, as well as having 'grippy' palms and fingers.

Amalgamating tape

This is a very useful piece of kit, as it allows you to make the shaft of the axe easier to grip. Purchased from electrical trade counters, it is a stretchy tape that adheres to itself; when wrapped around the shaft of the axe you can hold on without your glove slipping. It does tend to 'roll' up after some use, and requires replacing every now and then.

MOVEMENT SKILLS

There is a range of skills peculiar to dry tooling over and above those used for general climbing. Bear in mind that tooling is quite an intensive sport and that you should be well warmed up before taking on any of the more spectacular moves and sequences. Some normal bouldering followed by some traversing warm-ups on the dry tooling wall would be sensible.

Finding a good hold

This may sound easier than it actually is! Although you will obviously have a good grip on your ice axes, the tip of the pick is the bit that will be doing a lot of the load-bearing. Thus it needs to be placed securely onto a hold that will then allow you to use the axe in the way you need to. For instance, if the tip of the axe is placed on to a shallow hold and you move your weight upwards so that the load is more of an outwards pull than a downward one, the axe will fly off the placement.

- Before you place the tip of the axe, have a look at the hold. You may be used to the same type of hold on the climbing wall, so will know what to expect. However, you will be using it in a different manner so take care to load it properly. If you cannot see the area on to which the pick tip is being placed, move the pick slowly along the hold from left to right or front to back until you feel it hook onto the strongest point.

- Carefully put your weight on to the axe and feel for any movement in the tip. If there is none, you may be fine to fully load the placement and move on to the next one.

- Most placements will require you to maintain the same direction of loading on the axe shaft. Thus, if you are moving up and past a hold, keep the loading on it low by dropping your shoulder, elbow or complete body weight downwards, thus maintaining the same pull on the axe. Be aware that if the axe flies off from a hold it does it without any warning, so be prepared!

It will only be after quite some time on the wall that you'll start to get a feel for what will, and won't, be good placements. Once you have got a feel for the basics it will be time to move on to more interesting manoeuvres.

Matching

This is where both tools are placed on the same hold. It is very common when traversing as well as moving upwards, and allows you to use a good hold to its maximum advantage. For instance, if traversing from left to right, having moved the axe in your right hand to a good ledge, you 'match' tools on the same hold which allows you to then move off with the right tool again. This stops you having to make awkward crossover moves or reaching through to gain the next hold.

Stein pulls

Also known as 'can openers' – and one of the classic moves used by dry-toolers – these are very useful and come in a variety of forms. Basically, it involves using the tip of the pick on a hold and the top of the pick nearer to the shaft

A Stein pull; pulling down on the shaft will wedge the axe securely into place

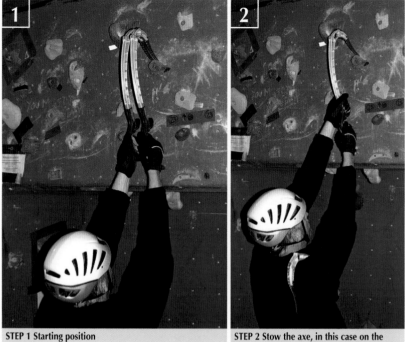

STEP 1 Starting position

STEP 2 Stow the axe, in this case on the shoulder, and match hands on the other axe

to lever on to another suitable surface, wedging the axe in place. Stein pulls can be used on vertical or horizontal ground with the axe being held in a variety of positions. They can be used to gain height as well as to get a rest, and as long as pressure is maintained on the shaft the axe should stay in place. Make sure that the holds being used are strong, as there is a huge pressure being exerted on them by the axe tip, especially when you are hanging upside down from the roof!

Swapping hands

The great advantage of leash-less climbing is that you are free to move around the wall almost as you like, with no restraining leashes keeping one hand locked on to one tool. For instance, if you were using leashes and had your right tool on one hold, with the next hold further off to the right, it would be quite tricky to reach across to it, and your balance would certainly be compromised. Without leashes, however, you stow the left tool, bring your left hand onto the right-hand axe, take your right hand off and retrieve the spare axe, and continue. This is better explained with a series of photographs.

STEP 3 Retrieve the axe and move to the next hold

The important thing to work out is what to do with the axe you are letting go of. There are a number of answers to this, but the following are the most common.

- Firstly, you could leave it in place on the wall or hang it on a suitable hold. Obviously, it needs to be positioned so that it is within reach and cannot be dropped, but you may find a hold over which you can hang it while changing hands.

- Secondly, you can use your shoulder as shown in the photographs (above). It will be best to have the axe shaft crossing your body diagonally, giving less chance of it falling off to the side and being lost. Also, make sure that the handle is in a position where you can easily grasp it again when needed.

- The third swapping method uses the thumb of the hand holding the axe shaft which is holding your weight. Move the free axe to your supporting hand and hook the pick over the crook of your thumb. Swap hands on the supporting axe and now move the pick up to the new hand, hooking it over this thumb. You can now move your free hand down to the axe grip and finish the sequence.

169

STEP 1 Hooking the free pick over the supporting thumb

STEP 2 Having swapped hands, the pick is now over the new supporting hand's thumb; the handle of the axe can now be grasped

Another possibility is to hook the pick of the axe needing to be stored into a hole or slot on the placed axe. This can sometimes make the axe a little difficult to retrieve once you have swapped hands, but is certainly an option.

Short-tooling

This is simply using the placed tool as something to pull up on in order to reach higher with the other tool. Stow the second axe (in this case the most useful place being over the shoulder) and place your spare hand on the axe shaft above the supporting hand. Pull up, retrieve the stored axe and place it on a higher hold.

Figure of four

This is not only one of the most spectacular techniques in dry tooling but is also one of the most useful. It is generally used when crossing areas of horizontal ground, such as a large roof, where you may need to hang from a single point while moving the free axe to another hold in order to progress.

The term is used when an opposing leg and arm are linked, with, for instance, your right leg being hooked over your left arm, or vice versa. It is a very technical position to get in to but, with perseverance, you will find that it

becomes possible to carry out one or more figure of fours in a sequence, useful for traversing roof problems.

Figure of four

- Find a suitable section of roof (it is not realistic to carry this out on a vertical wall), and have both your axes on good holds.
- Move your feet close to the axe heads, then bring one foot through and over the opposite arm, say right leg/ left arm (see photographs). Make sure that you get your knee over the crook of your elbow, as it will be more comfortable.
- The hardest part – apart from being flexible enough to finish the manoeuvre – is keeping a firm grip on the axe handle, so make sure that your supporting hand is comfortable and holding on tight.
- Once in the figure of four position, you can lift the right axe off its hold and move it on further to the next hold and repeat the process if need be.

Figure of nine

This is very similar to a figure of four, except this time the same side arm and leg (left and left or right and right) are used. Some climbers find it a useful technique when continuing on after a figure of four, as the leg that has been

Figure of nine over one arm can be moved across without having to drop it down as you bring the other up to complete a second figure of four. I find this quite tricky and would rather figure of four my way across a roof section, but try it out and see what works for you.

Resting

Dry tooling is really hard work! Any chance you get to rest and shake out should be taken. When climbing on slabs or steep walls this should not be too much of a problem. Simply have one axe on a good hold, carefully store the other and then shake out each arm in turn, swapping hands on the placed axe as and when you need to (another benefit of leash-less climbing). That's all well and good, but what about on roofs or overhanging ground? For steeper terrain a good method is to use a Stein pull.

- Find a suitable hold at around hip level and place the axe.
- Hook a leg over it, which will allow you to drop your arm down and shake out. If you are balanced correctly you may also be able to swap hands on the placed tool and rest the other arm for a while.

On roofs, the figure of four and figure of nine techniques will allow one arm to be rested at each move. Obviously the loading on the supporting arm will be quite high, but you will have a chance of gaining a bit of respite for the other.

GETTING PRACTICE

Practising dry tooling techniques, such as figures of four and nine, can be done almost anywhere. Some climbers have converted sections of their garages into dry tooling 'caves', where they can perfect certain techniques. Drilling pick-sized holes into the rafters is a quick and easy way of doing this. However, if you are thinking of doing something along similar lines, be very careful to give yourself ample matting. Falling when practising a figure of four, for instance, onto a concrete garage floor, would cause serious injury, particularly to your back and head. Bouldering mats are very good, and a lot of climbers scour the local papers for old mattresses that can be used to pad out the landing area.

Resting on a Stein pull

11 OTHER CLIMBING WALL ACTIVITIES

Climbing on an indoor ice wall

Apart from the obvious activity of climbing on the wall and dry tooling, facilities are increasingly offering other activities on site. Most large walls will have a shop and café, perhaps a gymnasium and hot tub, but you may find other forms of adventurous activity being offered as well.

ICE WALLS

Indoor ice climbing has become very popular in recent years, although the practicalities (and financial considerations) of building such a facility has meant that ice walls are nowhere near as common as indoor rock-climbing walls.

They generally resemble a large refrigerator (both in appearance and feel), usually with a series of windows for observation. These are kept to a minimum, however, as maintaining a constant temperature requires a good deal of insulation.

Most walls will have bottom ropes already set up, as placing ice screws is not generally allowed due to the soft nature of the ice. The ice is usually hand-packed onto the wall by staff at regular intervals; the busier the wall the more frequently it will need repacking.

There will usually be a limit to the number of people who can be on the wall at any one time, with other rules covering the use of wrist loops or lanyards (to avoid dropping axes onto your belayer or other users), as well each climber needing a helmet and some form of eye protection.

SKY RIDES AND HIGH ROPES

These activities often make the most of the available space high up in the roof of the building. This not only gives space to build suitable constructions but also serves to heighten the experience for participants!

Activities of this kind are very technical in nature and a high degree of skill is needed to design and construct the systems, all to industry standards. Personal safety is paramount and a number of systems will be in place to ensure that the session is as risk-free as possible.

Indoor high-ropes course at Ratho

Slack lining

SLACK LINING

This is a very popular form of entertainment, which is useful for climbers as it does a lot to help to build up balance and poise. A tape around 2 to 5cm wide is attached at both ends so that it hangs like a loose tightrope. You can balance on it, walk from end to end and even practise a variety of balancing tricks, such as turning on the spot, sitting down and standing back up, and so on.

Appendix 1
CLIMBER'S CHECKLIST

It is important to go through a mental checklist before climbing, be it bouldering, bottom-roping, leading or working with a group. The following items are the most important ones that should be considered, but the list is non-exhaustive – there will undoubtedly be more to add depending on the activity and situation. The cross-referencing is for guidance only, as there will quite naturally be a degree of overlap as well as your own interpretation.

	BOULDERING	BOTTOM ROPING	LEADING	GROUP SESSIONS
Rings and watches off	✓	✓	✓	✓
No breakable objects in pockets	✓	✓	✓	✓
No bulky objects in pockets	✓	✓	✓	✓
No sharp objects in pockets	✓	✓	✓	✓
Valuables secured	✓	✓	✓	✓
Harness off, or at least any karabiners etc off harness	✓			
Chalk bag off	✓			
Spotter correctly positioned	✓		✓	
Harness on and adjusted appropriately		✓	✓	✓
Buckles doubled back		✓	✓	✓
Helmet adjusted				✓
Rope through correct part of harness		✓	✓	✓
Correct main knot		✓	✓	✓
Correct stopper knot		✓	✓	✓

	BOULDERING	BOTTOM ROPING	LEADING	GROUP SESSIONS
Final knot correct size		✓	✓	✓
Knot tightened		✓	✓	✓
Bottom rope not twisted		✓		
Climber and belayer on appropriate side of rope coming from top anchor		✓		
Belay device threaded correctly		✓	✓	✓
Self-locking device test-tugged to check correct rope direction		✓	✓	✓
Belay device clipped into appropriate part of harness		✓	✓	✓
Belayer's stance correct		✓	✓	✓
Belayer's distance from wall correct		✓	✓	✓
Rope run through and close to hand		✓	✓	✓
Ground anchor correctly used		✓	✓	✓
ABC correct		✓	✓	✓
No kit lying around	✓	✓	✓	✓
No climbers in immediate vicinity and in any danger	✓	✓	✓	✓
Correct equipment on instructor's harness				✓
Group briefed				✓
Rest of group in safe area				✓
Grade of climb appropriate				✓
Lower-off practised low down				✓
Rope being dead-ended when peer belaying				✓

Appendix 2
ASSOCIATIONS
AND AWARD SCHEMES

Atmospheric climbing in a converted church, Glasgow

This appendix includes details about organisations that have connections to climbing walls. Full details of each organisation can be found on the relevant websites listed below.

MOUNTAIN LEADER TRAINING (MLT)

Mountain Leader Training
Hyfforddi Arweinwyr Mynydda

CWA, SPA and CWLA schemes
There are a number of climbing awards available in the United Kingdom, with the CWA, SPA and CWLA having particular relevance to indoor climbing. All of these are administered by Mountain Leader Training. All the schemes detailed require registration with the training board and consist of a training course (or in some cases exemption for very experienced candidates), a consolidation period and an assessment. Candidates are expected to have some experience prior to registration, and all relevant experience is entered into a logbook kept by the candidate. These awards are outlined below, and full details can be gained via the website at www.mltuk.org

Climbing Wall Award (CWA)
The scheme is for climbers who are in a position of responsibility when supervising climbing activities on indoor or

outdoor climbing walls, artificial boulders and towers. It is primarily concerned with ensuring good practice, leading to the safe enjoyment of climbing activities, and to an understanding of the sport. It covers the supervision and management of activities including bouldering, the teaching of basic movement skills and roped climbing and the avoidance of common problems, but excludes the teaching of leading. There is an add-on element, often run in conjunction with the standard course, which covers top-roping and abseil sessions.

- Training course duration: Minimum 12 hours (+ 4 hours for top-roping and abseiling module).
- Consolidation period: Recommended minimum of three months.
- Assessment course duration: Minimum 6 hours (+ 2 hours for top-roping and abseiling module).

Single Pitch Award (SPA)

The scheme is for those who are in a position of responsibility during single-pitch rock-climbing activities. It is primarily concerned with good practice, leading to the safe and quiet enjoyment of the activity. For the purposes of this scheme, a single-pitch route is one which is climbed without intermediate stances; is described as a single pitch in the guidebook; allows students to be lowered to the ground at all times; is non-tidal; is non-serious, having little objective danger and presents no difficulties on approach or retreat (such as route finding, scrambling or navigating). Topics covered include personal climbing skills, use of climbing walls, group climbing and abseiling, and the avoidance and solving of related common problems.

- Training course duration: 20 hours.
- Consolidation period: Recommended minimum of six months.
- Assessment course duration: 20 hours.

Climbing Wall
Leading Award (CWLA)

This scheme is for holders of the SPA or CWA awards who are in a position of responsibility when instructing and coaching the skills required to lead routes on indoor or outdoor climbing walls and towers, with fixed protection. It is primarily concerned with ensuring good practice, resulting in the safe development of leading skills, and to an understanding of the sport. It covers the introduction, coaching and ongoing development of the technical and movement skills required to lead routes safely. It excludes the skills associated with leading on natural crags and sport-climbing venues, such as placing protection (or using non-fixed pre-placed traditional protection) and the judgement required to lead routes on natural rock.

- Training course duration: 8 hours.
- Consolidation period: Recommended minimum of three months.
- Assessment course duration: 6 hours.

It is quite possible for those with reduced mobility to take part in well organised climbing sessions

NICAS

The National Indoor Climbing Achievement Scheme (NICAS) is a UK-wide scheme designed to promote climbing development and accredit individual achievement on artificial climbing structures. It can be used as a starting point for people wishing to take up climbing and mountaineering. It is open to all candidates aged seven and upwards.

The scheme is administered by the Association of British Climbing Walls Training Trust (ABCTT) and is recognised by the British Mountaineering Council, the Mountaineering Council of Scotland and the Mountaineering Council of Ireland.

Aims of the scheme
- To develop climbing movement skills and improve levels of ability.
- To learn climbing ropework and how to use equipment appropriately.
- To develop risk assessment and risk management skills in the sport.
- To work as a team, communicate with, and trust a climbing partner.
- To provide a structure for development, motivation and improved performance.
- To develop an understanding of the sport, its history and future challenges.
- To provide a record of personal achievement.
- To point the way to further disciplines and challenges in climbing beyond the scheme.

Structure of the scheme
The scheme comprises five levels of award aimed at complete novices to expert climbers. The scheme is split into two parts and takes a minimum of 100 hours to complete in its entirety. Part 1 contains Levels 1 and 2, and Part 2 contains Levels 3 to 5. Upon registering with an Awarding Centre candidates receive a log booklet for Part 1 and a log folder for Part 2. After achieving each level they are awarded with a certificate on behalf of the ABCTT.

The five levels are:

1 Foundation Climber
An entry level aimed at novices that recognises their ability to climb safely under supervision.

2 Top Rope Climber
Aimed at promoting good practice in climbing and bouldering unsupervised on an artificial wall.

3 Technical Climber
A more advanced top-roping and bouldering level that focuses on developing technique and movement skills.

4 Lead Climber
Concentrates on the skills required to both lead climb and belay a lead climber.

5 Advanced Climber
The top level that focuses on improving performance, a deeper understanding of climbing systems and the wider world of climbing.

For details of the scheme
visit the website at www.nicas.co.uk

ABC

The Association of British Climbing Walls (ABC) was formed in 1994 and meets three times a year to discuss and address the many issues and opportunities facing our industry. It is open to anyone who owns or operates a climbing wall, regardless of size. New and existing climbing walls are welcome as prospective members. Initially aspirant membership is available for one year. Full membership is available after one year for climbing walls operating in compliance with ABC guidelines.

The main objective of the ABC is 'The development and benchmarking of Safe Operating Practice and Quality Management Procedures for Artificial Climbing Structures'. This is achieved through extensive discussion and consultation with member walls, the Health and Safety Executive, the British Mountaineering Council (BMC) and the Climbing Walls Manufacturers Association (CWMA).

The safe operation and management of a climbing wall is a complex process where statutory requirements and duty of care are of paramount importance. The Association gives environmental health officers, insurers and climbing wall users the confidence that the highest standards of safety and operational procedures are practised at member walls.

The association oversees the running of the ABC Training Trust (ABCTT). This trust provides advice and training and is responsible for the National Indoor Climbing Achievement Scheme (NICAS).

Full information can be found at www.abcclimbingwalls.co.uk

Blindfolding a climber can help teach communication and efficient movement, as well as being fun. The blindfold should be removed for the descent.

THE BRITISH MOUNTAINEERING COUNCIL

The British Mountaineering Council represents climbers in the widest sense, which includes climbers' use of man-made climbing structures. The climbing wall industry has recently expanded at pace with over 400 climbing walls and over 40 dedicated climbing centres being used by climbers the length and breadth of Great Britain.

Since its creation the BMC Climbing Wall Committee has gathered information and promoted the use of climbing walls countrywide. The committee's main role is that of an expert advisory and facilitator group ensuring provision meets the demand of climbers wanting indoor facilities for training and recreation.

The committee comprises the Climbing Wall Representatives from the nine Areas of the BMC, who have a particular interest in climbing walls and, being active climbers themselves, have a good understanding of the sport. They have been elected by their area committee and thus represent that forum. These Area Representatives gather local information from prospective and existing wall providers and help with guidance on what climbers need, liaising with the BMC Climbing Wall Development Officer and their Area Committee on strategic issues. Others invited to attend the committee meetings include representatives from the CWMA, climbing wall operators, the English and Welsh Sports Councils, the Mountaineering Council of Scotland and the Mountaineering Council of Ireland.

The BMC National Council appoints a chairperson whose duty it is to oversee the work of the committee. A full-time development officer with special responsibility for climbing walls acts as committee secretary and offers support for all aspects of the work.

The activities of this committee include:

- Day-to-day practical advice given by the BMC office and by the Area Representatives to prospective or existing Project Managers.
- Advice to and liaison with official bodies – local authorities, HSE, Sports Council, Mountain Leading Training etc on matters related to climbing walls.
- Maintaining a paper directory and online database of walls.
- Providing help to the Area Committees in the preparation of regional strategic development plans.
- Coordinating and encouraging research into climbing wall matters.

BMC Climbing Wall Committee – Terms of Reference

- To provide advice on all aspects of climbing wall provision, location, design and management for any interested party.
- To act on behalf of all users in any matters involving climbing walls.
- To liaise with organisations such as the Association of British Climbing Walls (ABC), the Climbing Wall Manufacturers' Association (CWMA) and the Health & Safety Executive (HSE) regarding climbing wall issues.
- To gather and collate information on existing climbing walls for member enquiries, publications and future wall developments.
- To be a forum and support for local area representatives on climbing wall issues and development.

The BMC has recently produced the third edition of the *Climbing Wall Manual*, which covers technical climbing wall information aimed at designers, architects, leisure managers, facility owners and climbers.

For information on the climbing wall manual or any other climbing-wall-related issues please go to www.thebmc.co.uk/walls or contact walls@thebmc.co.uk.

MOUNTAINEERING COUNCIL OF SCOTLAND (MCofS)

The MCofS is the only recognised representative organisation for mountaineers who live in Scotland, and for everyone who enjoys walking and climbing in Scotland's mountains. MCofS is also the national governing body for the sport of competition climbing, known internationally as sport climbing.

It represents participants in all mountaineering activities – from occasional novice hillwalkers and inexperienced indoor climbers to elite athletes undertaking high altitude expeditions, cutting edge climbing ascents and competitions.

Founded in 1970 by the main Scottish clubs, the MCofS has over 10,000 members with 130 clubs affiliated and a network of over 900 volunteers.

It helps support youth climbing in Scotland with REALrock climbing sessions, coaching and competitions; supports adventure and sport climbing, competitions and expeditions through a Bursary; supports Scottish climbing walls through a walls network and the development of new walls; and it represents members' interests to government on issues concerning mountain safety, access and conservation.

You can join the MCofS as an individual or club member and become part of the future of Scottish mountaineering. See the website at: www.mcofs.org.uk.

Appendix 3
GLOSSARY

Abseiling Descending a rope under control, most commonly when using a descender device.

Arête An outside corner, such as the outside of an open book.

Ascender Device that clamps onto the rope and slides up, locking off when pulled downwards.

Auto-belay Automatic device that takes in the rope as the climber ascends and pays it out at a slow and constant rate when they fall or jump off.

Back-clipping Running the lead rope through a karabiner in the wrong direction.

Belaying Managing the rope in a manner that safeguards a climbing companion.

Bolt-on holds A common style of hold that is fixed to the wall with a bolt that screws into a threaded nut in the wall surface.

Bottom-roping Controlling the rope from the bottom of the wall.

Bouldering Solo climbing, commonly low down above matting, in order to practise moves or as part of training.

Bulge A section of wall that protrudes further out than the surrounding area.

Chalk Magnesium carbonate powder, used to dry fingertips and improve grip.

Corner An internal angle, similar to the inside of an open book.

Cow's tail Sling or similar attachment from an anchor to a harness as a safety back-up.

Dead-ending Loosely holding the dead rope coming from a novice's belay device as extra security.

Dead rope The rope held in the hand that is on the side of the belay device away from the climber.

Descender Device used for abseiling.

Direct belay A system where all the load is taken by the anchor, such as with some ground anchors or in top-rope and abseiling situations.

Dry tooling Using special axes to hook and pull on climbing holds.

Equalising anchors A system whereby two anchors are arranged so that each is sharing the load of a rig, abseiler and so on.

Extender Sewn tape with a karabiner at each end, or sometimes with one maillon, attached to the wall and through which the rope will run. Also known as a 'quick-draw'.

French Prusik Method of using a loop of rope to make a back-up on a climbing or abseil rope. Sometimes used during emergency procedures.

Friction Using rock-boot rubber or hands on the wall where no holds are present, such as on a slab, and relying on the friction thus created to keep the climber in place.

Ground anchor A place on the ground where a belayer can attach themselves, or from where a direct belay system can be set up, commonly when running a group session.

HMS A wide-ended karabiner that allows an Italian hitch to be used, often for belaying groups or in top-roping and abseiling situations. Also known as a 'pear-shape' karabiner.

In situ Equipment, most commonly extenders, that are already in place on the wall.

Jamming A style of hold where fingers or hands are wedged in a crack or narrow fissure. Can be secure but uncomfortable!

Jugs Large holds, also known as 'Thank God holds', as they often appear when most needed!

Leading The climber climbs the wall taking the rope up with them, clipping into extenders on the way.

Live rope The section of rope on the climber's side of a belay device.

Lower off To lower the climber down after they have ascended on a bottom rope or after leading. Also the name given to the karabiner and/or chain attachment at the top of the wall through which the rope is fixed.

Maillon A steel fixing with a screw sleeve that firmly closes the gap into which a rope or other object has been placed. Often used on technical rigs in place of a screwgate karabiner.

Overhang Section of wall that juts out over the rest.

Pear-shaped Another name for the HMS karabiner. (Also means that things have gone wrong!)

Peer belaying People with the same skill level managing each other's rope.

Prusik loop 50cm or so loop of 6mm rope with which a French Prusik can be tied.

Quick-draw Another name for an extender.

Resting Gaining a position on the wall whereby you can rest either one or both arms at a time.

Rigging rope A rope with low-stretch properties that is often used for abseiling and setting up systems. May also be used in some centres as a bottom rope. It should never be used for leading.

Roof Section of wall that juts out horizontally from the rest of the route.

Screw-on holds Commonly small holds, these can be fixed with wood screws in any position onto a wooden backing.

Screwgate Karabiner that has a sleeve which can be screwed shut to prevent the gate, through which the rope or other item has been passed, from opening accidentally.

Self-locking belay device Belay device that has an in-built method of clamping the rope, either with moving parts or with a passive 'rocking' action. Despite their name, these devices are absolutely not designed for hands-free use.

Sideways loading A karabiner that is being loaded across its narrowest plane, halfway down the back bar and across the gate. This weakens the karabiner considerably and should be avoided.

Slab A section of wall that is set back from vertical.

Spotting Safeguarding a boulderer or leader at the bottom of a climb by guiding them down to a safe landing area should they fall off.

Stepping through Placing a foot between the rope and the wall, mainly a problem with leaders. Falling like this can cause them to flip upside down.

Stretching Part of the preparation for climbing, stretching should be done in a very controlled manner and only when well warmed up.

Top-roping Method of controlling the rope from the top of the wall.

Warming down Light exercise at the end of a session to help avoid subsequent injury and stiffness.

Warming up Exercise regime at the start of a climbing session that can help with injury prevention and improved physical and mental performance.

Z-clipping When leading, clipping an extender with the rope from below the previous one. Moving up then becomes very awkward and opens the leader up to a long fall.

INDEX

LISTING OF CICERONE GUIDES

**BACKPACKING AND
CHALLENGE WALKING**
Backpacker's Britain:
  Vol 1 – Northern England
  Vol 2 – Wales
  Vol 3 – Northern Scotland
  Vol 4 – Central & Southern
      Scottish Highlands
End to End Trail
The National Trails
The UK Trailwalker's Handbook
Three Peaks, Ten Tors
BRITISH CYCLING
Border Country Cycle Routes
Cumbria Cycle Way
Lancashire Cycle Way
Lands End to John O'Groats
Rural Rides:
  No 1 – West Surrey
  No 2 – East Surrey
South Lakeland Cycle Rides
PEAK DISTRICT AND DERBYSHIRE
High Peak Walks
Historic Walks in Derbyshire
The Star Family Walks – The Peak
  District & South Yorkshire
White Peak Walks:
  The Northern Dales
  The Southern Dales
SUMMIT COLLECTIONS
Europe's High Points
Mountains of England & Wales:
  Vol 1 – Wales
  Vol 2 – England
Ridges of England, Wales & Ireland
The Relative Hills of Britain
IRELAND
Irish Coast to Coast Walk
Irish Coastal Walks
Mountains of Ireland
THE ISLE OF MAN
Isle of Man Coastal Path
Walking on the Isle of Man
**LAKE DISTRICT AND
MORECAMBE BAY**
Atlas of the English Lakes
Coniston Copper Mines
Cumbria Coastal Way
Cumbria Way and Allerdale Ramble
Great Mountain Days in the
  Lake District
Lake District Anglers' Guide
Lake District Winter Climbs
Lakeland Fellranger:
  The Central Fells
  The Mid-Western Fells
  The Near-Eastern Fells
  The Southern Fells
Roads and Tracks of the Lake
  District
Rocky Rambler's Wild Walks
Scrambles in the Lake District:
  Vol 1 – Northern Lakes
  Vol 2 – Southern Lakes

Short Walks in Lakeland:
  Book 1 – South Lakeland
  Book 2 – North Lakeland
  Book 3 – West Lakeland
Tarns of Lakeland:
  Vol 1 – West
  Vol 2 – East
Tour of the Lake District
Walks in Silverdale and Arnside
**NORTHERN ENGLAND
LONG-DISTANCE TRAILS**
Dales Way
Hadrian's Wall Path
Northern Coast to Coast Walk
Pennine Way
Reivers Way
Teesdale Way
**NORTH-WEST ENGLAND
OUTSIDE THE LAKE DISTRICT**
Family Walks in the
  Forest of Bowland
Historic Walks in Cheshire
Ribble Way
Walking in the Forest of Bowland
  and Pendle
Walking in Lancashire
Walks in Lancashire Witch Country
Walks in Ribble Country
**PENNINES AND
NORTH-EAST ENGLAND**
Cleveland Way and Yorkshire
  Wolds Way
Historic Walks in North Yorkshire
North York Moors
The Canoeist's Guide to the
  North-East
The Spirit of Hadrian's Wall
Yorkshire Dales – North and East
Yorkshire Dales – South and West
Walking in County Durham
Walking in Northumberland
Walking in the North Pennines
Walking in the South Pennines
Walks in Dales Country
Walks in the Yorkshire Dales
Walking on the West Pennine
  Moors
Walks on the North York Moors:
  Books 1 and 2
Waterfall Walks – Teesdale and
  High Pennines
Yorkshire Dales Angler's Guide
SCOTLAND
Ben Nevis and Glen Coe
Border Country
Border Pubs and Inns
Central Highlands
Great Glen Way
Isle of Skye
North to the Cape
Lowther Hills
Pentland Hills
Scotland's Far North
Scotland's Far West

Scotland's Mountain Ridges
Scottish Glens:
  2 – Atholl Glens
  3 – Glens of Rannoch
  4 – Glens of Trossach
  5 – Glens of Argyll
  6 – The Great Glen
Scrambles in Lochaber
Southern Upland Way
Walking in the Cairngorms
Walking in the Hebrides
Walking in the Ochils, Campsie
  Fells and Lomond Hills
Walking Loch Lomond and the
  Trossachs
Walking on the Isle of Arran
Walking on the Orkney and
  Shetland Isles
Walking the Galloway Hills
Walking the Munros:
  Vol 1 – Southern, Central and
      Western
  Vol 2 – Northern and Cairngorms
West Highland Way
Winter Climbs – Ben Nevis and
  Glencoe
Winter Climbs in the Cairngorms
SOUTHERN ENGLAND
Channel Island Walks
Exmoor and the Quantocks
Greater Ridgeway
Lea Valley Walk
London – The Definitive Walking
  Guide
North Downs Way
South Downs Way
South West Coast Path
Thames Path
Walker's Guide to the Isle of Wight
Walking in Bedfordshire
Walking in Berkshire
Walking in Buckinghamshire
Walking in Kent
Walking in Somerset
Walking in Sussex
Walking in the Isles of Scilly
Walking in the Thames Valley
Walking on Dartmoor
**WALES AND THE
WELSH BORDERS**
Ascent of Snowdon
Glyndwr's Way
Hillwalking in Snowdonia
Hillwalking in Wales:
  Vols 1 and 2
Lleyn Peninsula Coastal Path
Offa's Dyke Path
Pembrokeshire Coastal Path
Ridges of Snowdonia
Scrambles in Snowdonia
Shropshire Hills
Spirit Paths of Wales
Walking in Pembrokeshire
Welsh Winter Climbs

For full and up-to-date information on our ever-expanding list of guides, please visit our website:
www.cicerone.co.uk.

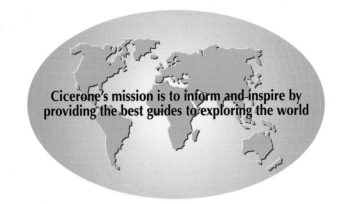

Cicerone's mission is to inform and inspire by providing the best guides to exploring the world

Since its foundation 40 years ago, Cicerone has specialised in publishing guidebooks and has built a reputation for quality and reliability. It now publishes nearly 300 guides to the major destinations for outdoor enthusiasts, including Europe, UK and the rest of the world.

Written by leading and committed specialists, Cicerone guides are recognised as the most authoritative. They are full of information, maps and illustrations so that the user can plan and complete a successful and safe trip or expedition – be it a long face climb, a walk over Lakeland fells, an alpine cycling tour, a Himalayan trek or a ramble in the countryside.

With a thorough introduction to assist planning, clear diagrams, maps and colour photographs to illustrate the terrain and route, and accurate and detailed text, Cicerone guides are designed for ease of use and access to the information.

If the facts on the ground change, or there is any aspect of a guide that you think we can improve, we are always delighted to hear from you.

Cicerone Press
2 Police Square Milnthorpe Cumbria LA7 7PY
Tel: 015395 62069 Fax: 015395 63417
info@cicerone.co.uk www.cicerone.co.uk